D1097645

Sweet & Salty
Memoirs & Musings

MARGARET ANN MARCROFT

The Memoirs and Musings of Margaret Ann Marcroft
ISBN 978-1-953120-24-3
Printed and bound in the U.S.A
Copyright © 2021 Margaret Ann Marcroft

ALL RIGHTS RESERVED

Edited by Catherine Marcroft
Cover design by Janet Marcroft
Design and production by Patricia Hamilton
Photos from the Marcroft archives

Published by
Keepers of Our Culture
an imprint of Park Place Publications
Pacific Grove, California

Dedicated to my parents,
Arthur and Frances Hutcheson,
whose example of good living
continues unto the fourth generation

CONTENTS

JOHN H. RICH, President.   CHARLES J. SARGENT, Cashier.
CARL F. HJERMSTAD, V.Pres.&Mngr.   EMIL L. LEE, Asst. Cashier.

THE

Goodhue County National Bank

CAPITAL $150,000
SURPLUS & PROFITS $100,000

Red Wing, Minn.   Oct. 25th. 1909

Mr. W. V. Hutcheson,

      Porterville, Cal.

Dear Sir;-

      We have to-day closed with Mr. A. H. Dicke the sale of your farm to him and have to report as follows;-

Paid your note given for interest on $2,900. mortgage to April 4th. 1909, canceled note enclosed,	$ 174.
Interest on same	5.90
Interest on $2,900. April 4th. to date	97.67
Mortgage assumed by A. H. Dicke, balance	2,900.00
Paid last half taxes, receipt enclosed,	22.52
Paid for abstract, receipt enclosed,	17.75
For drawing deed	1.
Allowed A. H. Dicke for clover seed	8.50
" " for surveying done	2.
" " for shingling porch	5.
" " ½ repairs on wind mill & pump	2.
Paid Mr. O'Reilly	6.
Exchange on enclosed draft and our services	7.50
Chicago draft herewith to balance	6,704.16

Purchase price of land	$9,600.	
Rent for 1909	360.	$9,960.00

      Kindly acknowledge receipt.

                   Yours truly,

                            Cashier.

Deed for the land in Minnesota.

CHAPTER ONE

THE DECADES

With the onslaught of the COVID-19 pandemic, I am reminded of the repercussions the Spanish flu pandemic had on our family. I remember hearing stories about how that event influenced my upbringing. Stories I remember, of course, are salvaged from the mental faculty called Memory. To quote one author I recently read, "Memory's trick is convincing you she speaks only the truth," or the "only" truth, so reader beware.

In 1918 my dad turned sixteen and so was still too young to volunteer for the army, much to his disgust! In the fall of that year, he was enrolled in California Polytechnic School at San Luis Obispo, which opened "October 1, 1903 for 20 students, offering secondary level courses of study, which took three years to complete." Naturally Dad boarded, taking the train from Porterville to San Luis Obispo. In 1910 Dad's folks, Margaret and Walter Hutcheson, had migrated from Minnesota, where Grandpa sold his inherited quarter of a section of grain land with dairy in order to take up orange farming in Porterville, California. They arrived with three children, and by 1918 had seven; my dad, Arthur Vincent, was the oldest.

Dad loved being at Cal Poly, especially his roommate who, according

Dad at Cal Poly.

to the stories, was something of a standup comic. At Christmas all the boys went home for the holidays. In early January 1919, Dad returned to school. No sooner had he arrived, than so did a telegram telling him to pack up everything and come home. His father, 41, and his brother, Jay, just younger than Dad, had died on the same day of the Spanish flu. Dad and his mother were to struggle to feed themselves and his siblings, as well as to educate the remaining five, leaving no time or energy for Dad to ever go back to school. Dad took up this challenge with only one act of rebellion: he started smoking!

The motto Cal Poly operated on was, "Learn by doing." In just one semester, Dad learned it well. He boarded in Duvell Hall. In the picture at left Dad is standing in front of the building at age sixteen. My brother Vince also boarded in this building during his sophomore year, 1947-1948, after which it was torn down to make room for newer buildings. Two of Vince's boys graduated from this school as did three of his grandsons and our daughter, Janet, so the school is well remembered in our family.

A month before Dad's 28th birthday my parents married in Visalia, California. Dad's mother, Grandmother Hutcheson, and youngest sister, Eleanor, moved to Fresno where Grandma ran a boarding house and put Eleanor through high school as she would have been about fourteen at the time of the wedding.

Mom, Frances Eloise Chambers, was a good match for Dad as far as being responsible. She

Grandma and Grandpa Chambers, 1930s.

3

Grandma Chambers and Mom's
brother Lawrence.

was born in Kansas, the third in a family of five. She had an older sister, brother, and two younger sisters. Her family had migrated to California in 1918 when Mom was half way through high school. Grandpa had run his own blacksmith shop successfully until he chose to invest in the White Tractor Company at the same time John Deere started making tractors. He had recently built a beautiful two-story brick home where Grandma taught piano. To their dismay, they lost all and were one of those who drove across half the nation to California in their car. Gertrude, their eldest, had secured a teaching job and stayed behind.

Mom started Visalia High as a junior and joined the basketball team, which traveled throughout the Central Valley. We still have her block V letter in that sport. Upon graduation, she secured a job in the courthouse at the Assessor's Office, which she held for ten years. Grandpa Chambers never really quite recovered from his bankruptcy, and welding jobs were few and far between, often leaving Mom the main bread winner. When her older brother, Lawrence, died of consumption–tuberculosis, Mom was stuck with the funeral bill or so I've been told. Since her two younger sisters married immediately out of high school, Mom footed a great deal of their wedding expenses as well.

The family may have chosen to settle in Visalia for any number of reasons: 1) it seemed the prettiest town in the San Joaquin Valley at the time with its many fruit orchards, 2) the several cannaries paid good wages, or 3) Mom's Aunt Myra and Uncle Will had already settled there. Aunt Myra and Uncle Will had a house on the edge of town where the large quilting frame took up most of the "great-room" and an apartment above the garage where Mom's grandmother lived for a short time. I only remember visiting her once and being served a huge cup—as big as a soup bowl—of hot milk with butter and pieces of toast floating in it. Food memories tend to stick. On the property were three fruit trees that we never had at the ranch—mulberry, fig and loquat.

Mom's Garden Street house.

Mom's folks bought a house on Garden Street, which several of us Hutchesons visited at the time of Mom's funeral in 1982. As of this writing it is still there. Since I was the first grandchild on both sides, there are several pictures of me on that porch or in the yard; but I'm getting ahead of the story.

Dad in the Sierras.

Mom and Dad both belonged to a church group of young people who hiked the Sierras in summer and took snow trips in the winter. Mom participated in community theatre after work. She had a beautiful voice and loved to dance — as did Dad. In fact, he often was chosen to judge ballroom dance contests in Visalia, all the rage at the time.

Mom, fifth from the left.

Frances Eloise Chambers, Mom at 24.

MEMORIES OF MOM

My very first memory is of living at the "Freitas" house across the road. The next memory is of moving to the ranch in 1935 when I was almost 4. The house was not much to brag about, but the folks were so excited. I remember Dad sweeping the "great room" out with a push broom, because they were having friends over to celebrate with a dance. Mom loved to dance; before she married she had been in quite a few community musicals where she sang and danced.

Another party woke me up one summer night with all the laughter and squealing. Several couples had been invited to go frog hunting with gigs in the big Tulare ditch. The men had parked their cars so the headlights shone on the water and after they had enough for a meal, they brought them to the house for the women to fry. I got to taste the frog legs and still like eating them. Also, frequently the folks would have Mom's sisters and their husbands over to dinner. Mom loved parties and having her sisters around, but neither Mom nor Dad were too fond of the brothers-in-law. Uncle Scottie also liked music, so he and Mom would sing, but when they all left Dad would always say, "I got the BEST of the Chambers' girls."

The folks also liked to play cards; usually with the Peltzers, Leonard and Geneva. We kids played "Kick the Can" 'till it was time for dessert. We ran through the orchards for hours even when it was pitch dark; no one seemed to notice. Then we would all pile into the Ford and drive home on the country roads from Ivanhoe to our house, trying to decide if we were following the moon or it was following us.

Mom was very energetic, social and optimistic. When we lived at the Freitas house Mom lost the diamond out of her engagement ring and it was never found. One Christmas when I was 9 or 10 we had a dusting of snow over the Christmas holidays—very rare! And that Christmas Dad had the diamond replaced in Mom's ring, between the sapphires. She was thrilled when she opened her Christmas present and I thought the whole event very romantic.

Mom spent a lot of her energy fixing three hot meals a day for years, and in the spring and summer she could be found painting or wall–papering our house except for the one summer she worked at the peach grading table along with us and the Mexican Braceros, while Aunt Myra cooked the noon meal and took care of Dorothy, the baby at the time.

It was about that time that Dad thought it would be helpful if Mom learned to drive the tractor. Frank, our live-in help could not drive, and we were too young. Dad brought the tractor up to the house and we children were admonished to stay on the porch that ran around the house and was about 6 feet across. Mom drove a gear shift car, but tractors were different, noisy for one thing and coordinating the gears and gas with your hands (not feet) was just foreign to her. The tractor roared so loud she could not hear the instruction Dad was giving and then we children were all yelling and running up and down the porch acting like she was going to run into us. She did have trouble stopping the thing. After a couple of tries Mom got off the tractor and said she was finished — and she was.

I really didn't spend much time with Mom as I hated being indoors, was somewhat of a tomboy, and started my first summer job after 8th grade. I never was willing to learn cooking or sewing from her. My loss! I did inherit her energy, optimism and love of music and children. Living on the farm and missing out on the cultural events was hard for her but I do not ever remember her complaining. Mom also was deeply devoted to her faith and we frequently said the rosary at night after dinner. She and I went to the Stations of the Cross on Friday evenings during Lent. It was our social outing. I am still grateful for the faith practices she taught me.

I delighted in spending a week or two in the summer at the Fitzgerald's cabin and then the summer after my eighth grade graduation I lived at Aunt Peggy's as I spent all day and night taking care of the Hipwell children while she worked at the cafeteria attached to their country store across from the Visalia Cannery.

In my junior year of high school I transferred to Immaculate Heart High School in Hollywood, so was only home in the summer when I worked at the Assessor's office in Visalia, where Mom had worked before she married. After high school I went to College of Sequoias for two years, but always worked in Uncle George and Aunt Peggy's mom and pop grocery in the summer and on weekends. During those two years, there were no girls' sports teams so I sang in the musical the school put on each year, which meant lots of nights out to practice. The next fall I left to finish my education at San Jose State.

From left—Mom, Gertrude, Catherine, and Margarite.

Is it any wonder I did not feel I knew my mom very well as, right out of college, I proceeded to teach school two years, marry and have a family. I admired and enjoyed Mom but really tried hard not to get caught up in working in the house. Maybe I secretly knew I was destined to spend the biggest chunk of my life doing exactly what Mom had done, but I had to teach myself, as I had not allowed myself to learn from her. I never could make fruit pies as fast as she could.

Dad had always envisioned building a new house on the ranch for Mom and finally did in the summer of 1956. My second child, Michael, was born in August and that month they moved in. I think Mom was grateful but exhausted by the whole venture. Again, I did not get to share her feelings at that time as I was too busy. We never really did connect again until I brought her to Katherine's Convalescent Hospital for the last four years of her life, where she died of Alzheimer's Disease during Holy Week, 1982. I saw her almost every day during those four years, feeding her the noon meal, but catching up by means of conversation could never really happen.

I WISH I WAS A ROCK

There are some things one just has had enough of. Robert Frost complains of too much apple picking, and that long after he is done, the memory of it causes him sleepless nights. I feel the same way about cooking! I keep hearing the familiar sound, not of apples rolling into the bin, but of voices asking "What's for dinner?" And do I know? Who says I must? Sometimes I'd rather just sit and collect dust.

My mother had a poem framed and hanging on the kitchen wall — "I Wish I Was a Rock." I thought it funny at first, then odd, as I read it each day as I passed it. Why would Mom want to be a rock? The author was anonymous so it wasn't like it was written by a friend or relative that she wanted to honor.

Raising my family, cooking was my least favorite activity. Trying to balance meat, carbohydrate, leafy greens or other vegetables plus a fruit or baked dessert all in one meal seven times a week for nine of us for years didn't interest me at all. But why should I complain? Mom did it twice a day for more of us for more years, plus a full breakfast, and she never complained. This last twenty years, things have changed for me. There are no longer children at home and we are sometimes not home either at meal time in which case we eat out or skip a meal, but somehow the question persists, "What's for dinner, or shall we eat out?" With dietary restrictions, it is sometimes easier to eat at home.

Don't misunderstand me—family gatherings around the table are more precious than any other ritual to me—it was just the planning and working with food, that commodity that seems to disappear instantly after hours of preparation, that seems tedious. I finally see why that poem was so important to Mom. When Mom and Dad moved into the new house, after I'd married and left home, somehow the poem got lost. Now I'm thinking of having it done in calligraphy and framed for my kitchen wall.

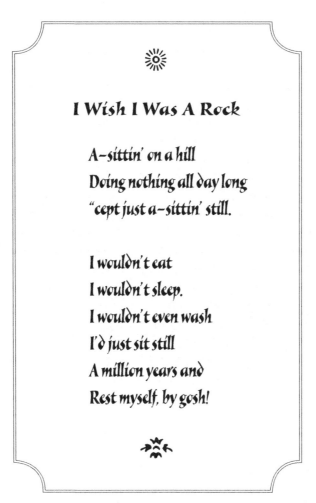

I Wish I Was A Rock

A-sittin' on a hill
Doing nothing all day long
"cept just a-sittin' still.

I wouldn't eat
I wouldn't sleep.
I wouldn't even wash
I'd just sit still
A million years and
Rest myself, by gosh!

Arthur Vincent Hutcheson. Dad at about 24 years old.

MEMORIES OF DAD

Levis, blue denim work shirts and red handkerchiefs—slacks, dress shirts and ties.

When we were young, we sometimes formed our image of our parents by what they wore and sometimes by all the things they did. I remember a dad who was always up before me and readily available in the fields. I remember a man who held us when we were wracked with whooping cough, and taught us to swim by throwing us upstream in the river to catch us as the current carried us back to him. He was a man who loved to dance and took us to father-daughter dances and dance lessons, and when once he and I had to walk the last two miles home as he had run out of gas. He could also stand by you when you were in pain. I had each arm set, one year after the other, and disinfected my ankle with iodine after I ran into the mower sickle. He removed a fish bone from my sister Eileen's throat with long needle-nosed pliers borrowed from the neighbors—with four pairs of anxious eyes standing at his side.

My earliest memory of Dad is of the times we spent together. My favorite possession was a child's wicker rocker so light I could carry it. Most evenings after dinner Dad liked to go sit on the "throne" and read the paper which came just before dinner. In this house the bathroom was one of the few rooms with a door that would shut and lock (though we children were forbidden to lock it). I would carry my chair in and a book and as Dad sat on the toilet, I sat in front of him and "read" my book. We didn't talk or interact, just spent time together. He worked in the fields or on Highway 198 construction crew, so when I could get him alone, I took advantage of it.

One summer day Dad came to the back door in very muddy boots as we were all playing on the porch. He asked me to go get Mother from the back of the house as he wanted to speak to her. I turned and yelled, "Mom, Dad wants to talk to you." He quietly said, "I could have done that. Now walk back and get her." He taught lessons with a quiet emphasis that made you remember them.

Dad was generous to a fault! He gave tractor–trailer rides to about a hundred kids in an afternoon, as he and Mom hosted the end of the year choir picnics for several years. Being the oldest in his family he often had his sisters' families to the farm for holidays, as they lived in town and the houses were too close together to really holler, laugh and argue over politics and religion. Dad frequently made a freezer of ice cream, which he seemed to churn in the blink of an eye. He made one for our 8th grade end of year party and when he brought it, Sr. Alphonsus said, "Thank you, dear," and Dad turned beet red. He turned the ice cream freezer for the ditch day party I'd organized in junior college for the P.E. majors, and loaned me the keys to his pickup to go to the river that day. Another time he gave me gas for my boyfriend's car when we ran out and had to walk back to the ranch.

Dad seemed always the one to take us to the doctor. When I was thirteen, the folks decided the four oldest of us would have our tonsils out on the same day. It was the trend to have children's tonsils out. All four of us went with Dad early one morning to surgery. Since I had a toothache (two molars were really in need of attention) Dad asked Dr. Wise to remove them while I was under the anesthetic and he did! I awoke minus the toothache, but had a very sore throat!

Punishment for bad behavior was Dad's rule, but he was capable of reversing his decision. The Fuller brush man had just come and with all these girls and their long hair Mom had bought a nice brush with a long handle. It was lying on the dining room table and when the folks stepped out Vince picked it up, brandishing it like a weapon. We were all running from him and yelling. He brought the brush down on the edge of the dining room table. The handle promptly broke off! Dad was so upset he sent Vince to his room and said he would have no dinner as it was almost that time. Fran, Bill, Eileen and I all began to plead and cry (I guess thinking Vince would starve to death). Dad relented and let Vince have dinner with us. We were all very relieved.

Dad could be equal parts tease and encourager when I embarked on projects that I loathed to finish. We all got the impression that we had to do things in and with our lives that mattered, at least I did. Dad and Mom had done so much for us that we wanted to do for them. He did accomplish a lot with his eighth-grade education, from raising and educating his five siblings after his dad died when he was sixteen, to loving and educating the eight of us. Along the way he purchased one hundred acres, twenty to forty at a time, built a new house after twenty-six years of marriage living in a house built in the 1800s that came with few amenities. His focal point was always doing right by God, so neighbors who chided him for his faith were hard to take. I dare to guess the hardest part as he grew older and after his esophageal cancer, was letting go — learning to let God do for him.

Spending time with Dad meant getting to share his possessions and the responsibilities that went with them. One other picture of Dad in my mind's eye is of the long summer evenings when he sat on bales of hay (no yard furniture) in the front yard reflecting on his day. Dad was very spiritual, though he never talked about God, you knew he was talking to Him.

Clockwise, Eleanor, Gertrude, Margaret, Buster (Pete), Arthur (Dad), and Larry, 1922.

The last three months of his life after a medical procedure went wrong, we had him in a rest home near my sister's home in Marin. Mom had developed Alzheimer's disease, and he had been taking care of her (with help) for two years. I went to visit him at the rest home once. He said he wanted to talk to a priest. I said I would go next door to the rectory and get one. But he impatiently said, "No Father is right there", pointing to the corner of the room. I saw no one but he did! I left so they could converse.

On Thanksgiving 1976, my sister brought him to her house for dinner and on taking him back to the rest home that evening, she said he stopped at every room (some 20) on the way to his room. He shook hands with the men and doffed his hat to the women—smiling all the while, according to my sister. When he got to his room, and my sister, nurse Fran, had safely tucked him into bed, he went to sleep and did not awaken.

I usually felt a close bond with my dad, especially on the nights he would awaken me to accompany him to Adoration of the Blessed Sacrament from 1 a.m. to 2 a.m., as each of the Knights of Columbus signed up for one of the twenty-four hours each year. I felt honored and I think on that Thanksgiving night he was honoring each of God's creations as he moved down the hall to his room. It was from him that I learned that everyone created matters. Yes, we are created to use our gifts to glorify God, but we are also created to let others see how great God's love is for each and every one of His creations. It's about the two halves of life; the doing half and the being half. Eventually we discover it is not what we do for God but what God has done for us.

From left—Margaret (Peggy), Pete, Grandma Hutcheson, Eleanor, Dad (Arthur), Gertrude, and Larry, 1930.

From left—Peggy, Larry, Arthur, Eleanor (Sister Olivia), Gertrude, and Pete.

Gratitude

Gratitude, it has been said

Is the heart of prayer—an attitude –

Where to start—"Our Father who art"?

Graces abound; be they of faith, food or friends.

The key is in recognition; followed by the admission

that nothing I've said or done; imagined or created,

Has deserved, earned or fully desired

All my multiple, ongoing, inexplicable gifts,

Be they relationships, qualities, or possessions,

These freely given endowments flood my senses.

And leave me very thankful, yet wondering

Barefoot Days

Crisp cool powdery dust
Lightly covers our faire bare feet
As we walk to the swimming hole.

Hours of splashing, laughing, shouting
Oblivious of the sun.
Time to head back home to lunch.

Noonday sun; no shoes in sight
Trees' shadows few and far between
Children run from shade to shade.

Plentiful puncture vines are in the
Blistering, burning dusty shoulder
Beside the melting asphalt country road.

A few yards at a time
Excruciating pain
How far to the next spot of shade?

Again, pick a spot
All together now, RUN!
Dad's car! Shouts of joy!

Seared flesh ... Dad's disgust

Mom and Dad's wedding photo.

CHAPTER TWO

THE THIRTIES

On May 17, 1930 my folks married at St. Mary's, Visalia, a small stone church (appropriately) on Church Street. Dad's sisters, Margaret and Gertrude, provided a small reception.

Mom continued her job at the court house. They lived outside Tulare on a dairy farm where Dad was employed and where I was born. They lived there until I was 2 and 1/2 or so. About the time my brother Vince was born we moved to what we later called the

I was born July 8, 1931.

Freitas House. Then, in 1935, they moved across the road onto their own 40 acres with house, prune orchard, and alfalfa fields.

The story goes that on the day of my arrival, July 8, 1931, the temperature was 120 degrees, and Grandma Hutcheson (still living with Mom and Dad) hung a wet sheet over the doorway with an electric fan blowing the damp air on Mom in the bedroom. There was a doctor in attendance but Mom said later he was drunk, so no help at all. Apparently, I was very dry and shriveled when I was born, so my nickname was "Prune."

The other story I remember is that sometime during my second year, my Grandmother Chambers was killed in an automobile accident in the under pass between Hanford and Visalia. Alcohol was involved as Grandpa was quite a drinker. These were hard times for Mom, I imagine.

Me with my favorite stuffed animal.

My first memories are at the "Freitas" house. I had a wicker rocker just my size and a stuffed horse, red with white polka dots, that went wherever I went.

One vivid memory was of being put in the wash tub on the back porch to be washed down (I'm sure I was good and dusty) when I stood up and stuck my finger into a naked light socket hanging above the tub. I screamed, and Mom came running.

A story I was told was of a house warming for the folks at this same house. Mom's dad lived with us for a while, and made beer to pass the time. He hid the bottles under the bed, and when a string of cars with their lights out came up the drive to surprise the folks one night, they were sure it was the "law" as this was Prohibition time. Luckily, they were friends, celebrating the folk's move from the Tulare farm. I soon brought out a bottle from where my two-year old self had seen Grandpa hide it. Others had brought their own bottles.

>⌒⌒⌒<

In 1935, Dad and Mom, my brother Vince and I moved to the house across the road where I lived until I left home. Vince was born in Kaweah

Me, approximately 2½ years old.

Hospital in Visalia and was still small enough to be moved in a dresser drawer. The house seemed huge, a kitchen, one bathroom with a giant bathtub on claw feet, room for three at a time, a great room and four bedrooms—two on each side of a hallway six feet wide. The whole house was surrounded by a six-foot wide porch, half screened in, half open. I do remember riding my tricycle round and round on the outside porch and singing to the moon. I also remember Dad sweeping out the great room with a push broom and scattering "spangles" on the wood floor. These were white thinly sliced chips of soap to make the floor slick for dancing. All their friends came to celebrate their house warming.

My first memories of the ranch were mostly of outside time—in the dirt and irrigation ditches in the summer and on that porch in the winter, when the Tulare River that ran through the ranch sometimes flooded. Each of the four bedrooms had at least one big window, some had two, none with screens, perfect for climbing in and out of when we were supposed to be napping or when sent to our room.

The country school, called Deep Creek, was a quarter to a third of a mile toward Exeter on highway 198. It was a two-room school for grades 1 through 8. Mrs. Bower taught the upper grades, and Mrs. Devine taught the lower four. I walked to and from. For the first week, a couple of 6th - 7th grade girls walked me to school, then I was on my own. That first year, I caught all the childhood diseases known to kids (except mumps—got them as a freshman in high school and shared them with Dad and siblings). I missed so much school with impetigo, ring worm, measles, whooping cough, chicken pox and scarlet fever that my teacher brought me books to read (learn from) at home. I was passed to second grade on probation. By that time, besides me and Vince, there was sister Fran and brother Bill, and I shared everything with all of them. I still remember feeling the fear of not recovering my breath when coughing, but by May, I was well enough to be in the play at the end of the year. I played the part of some eighth grade girl's doll and walked the stage stiff-legged; my only line was "Mama", "Mama." The year ended on a high.

Second grade was memorable for three reasons:

1) Having to stay after school for helping a fellow student with his combinations, giving him the answers of my test (a no-no),

2) Writing my combinations with chalk on the shiny black trunk of Dad's first "new" car, a '38 or '39 Ford sedan. I hadn't heard Dad walking up from the field for lunch, and got my bare legs switched good — I screamed and Mom and Grandma Hutcheson came running. I don't remember Dad ever spanking anyone again. Grandma lived with us short of a year or so till her bone cancer got so bad she had to live with Dad's sisters in Visalia. Some days, I took her breakfast in bed, then because of her illness and no appetite, I ate most of it.

3) Seeing a neighbor boy, Tony, whipped with a razor strop by the principal in front of class; he had started throwing erasers when the teacher left for a few minutes. He never shed a tear, but I sat at the back and wept until my teacher diverted my attention with a job, making mimeographed copies of math exercises using a gelatinous mixture in a tray.

Most of my memories of the rest of the thirties and the first half of the forties are wrapped and entwined with my stories of the people in my life: Mom, Dad, aunts and uncles, Grandma Hutcheson and Grandpa Chambers, Aunt Myra, Emma, Frank, cousins and others. I include them here and will pick up the "Decades" later. By my ninth birthday, Grandma Hutcheson and Grandpa Chambers had passed on. My parents had housed and fed for months to years most of the others including Aunt Myra, Frank, my dad's brothers and youngest sister, Eleanor. On October 6, 1944, my youngest sister Elizabeth arrived, completing our family of eight children, five girls and three boys: Margaret, Vincent, Frances, Bill, Eileen, Dorothy, Patrick and Elizabeth, in order of birth.

Let me first begin by talking about our house, which did seem to have a personality of its own.

The majestic oak tree.

OUR HOUSE

It sat between two majestic valley oaks that were two hundred or more years old and about 200 to 250 feet high. The house was a long rectangular shape that ran north and south with the trees flanking the east and west thus providing both morning and afternoon shade. The lowest branches were at least forty feet off the ground, so safe from us kids as no one could get a foothold nor could one child encircle either of them with their arms.

I never really looked at the outside of the house I grew up in, until Uncle Al took the picture of us leaving on our honeymoon with the house in the background. It was built in 1898, all wood, and had vines covering the outside. This was June 26, 1954. We had moved here in 1935.

Our wedding day, June 26, 1954.

31

Left to right: Back row—Fran, Mom, Vince, Dad.
Front row—Dorothy, Elizabeth, Eileen, and Bill.
Patrick is in front.

I remember the porches, outside and inside. The outside porch was for drying walnuts, riding tricycles, jumping off onto the lawn, sitting and weaving Mary crowns from the Cecil Brunner rose bush in May and relaxing while sucking the honey from the honeysuckle bush all spring. It was for playing on when flood waters and mud circled three feet below, several years

Dad with Fran, Vince, and me.

32

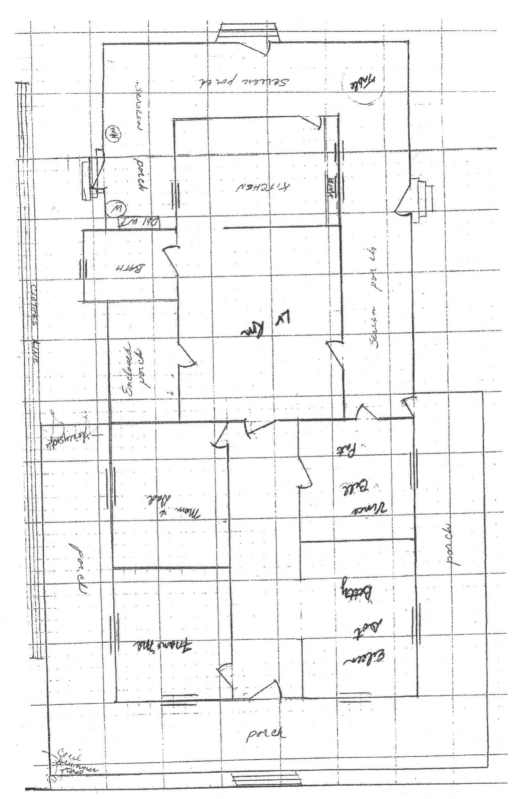

The floor plan of our house.

running. It was for climbing out onto from bedroom windows when we were supposed to be asleep in the summer.

The inside porch was for reclining on old wicker furniture, as I read the "Oz" series of books to Vince, Fran and Bill on hot summer days while Mother sewed clothes for the next school year or mended. It was for doing the wash and collecting it to take out and hang on the line while Mom and I sang all the light opera songs she could teach me. It was for dinner on hot days, entertaining on my thirteenth birthday, as well as a place to bring my junior college friends. It was a place where Mother fed the "Knights of the Open Road" — homeless men who roamed the roads of California in 1930s — in the winter!

Inside, the kitchen was for cooking, first by wood stove then electric; it was where we ate breakfast, lunch and dinner in the fall, winter and spring. The bathroom, just off the great room near the kitchen, was to wash, bathe and use the toilet; hair and makeup were to be taken care of in the bedrooms as there were ten of us and only one bathroom, except for my brother Bill who tied up the room for many minutes combing his pompadour.

The great room (ahead of its time) was for gathering, talking, entertaining company — whole families at a time — games, singing around the piano and naps. It held a huge pot-bellied oil stove for heat, replaced by a floor furnace years later. In the winter we grabbed our clothes each morning and headed to dress around the big stove. The rule, as I remember, was "No one ate breakfast till all had on shoes and socks" so the four older children dressed the four younger quickly. In the summer doors to both side porches, which were enclosed, were opened to create a breeze and Dad took a nap after the noonday meal for about 30 minutes on the floor. The great room opened at one end into the kitchen and at the other end into a hallway six feet wide and about forty feet long. At first the hallway contained our windup Victrola and a buffet than didn't fit in the great room. Later, it was where Aunt Myra slept during her last illness. Between my sophomore and junior years, the great room also held the party line phone. No privacy there. It held the radio console too where Dad listened to the news every morning before work and we listened to the Tom Mix, Little Orphan Annie and Lone Ranger serials every weekday late afternoon, usually while folding clothes.

The long hallway had two bedrooms off each side and a door at the end to the outside unscreened porch. This door had a twist doorbell and faced steps down to the ground. We thought that was originally the front door, as the first bedroom on the right had French doors; perhaps it had been a parlor. At any rate the French doors didn't last long and when gone that bedroom just had no doors. As things gradually changed, the steps were removed and the door locked. Eventually an oil heater was placed at the end of the hall in front of the door, to heat the bedrooms. Each bedroom originally had wallpaper with cheesecloth backing applied over wood walls. All the ceilings were twelve feet high and the baseboards were ten inches high.

One night while the folks were out briefly my brothers got into a peanut butter fight flinging spoons full of peanut butter from the ends of dinner knives at each other. Needless to say, some of the gobs landed on the walls and ceilings so ladders were required in the clean-up process. Difficult! When the folks came home and saw the mess, Mom didn't skip a beat on her way to bed –"Clean it up" — she said and left the room.

Mom was adamant about improving the looks of this old house so every spring she set about painting and wallpapering. We delighted in new linoleum where it was so easy to play jacks for hours or in the new

Aerial of the ranch off Highway 198.

linoleum tiles in the great room which were much easier to clean than the wood floor. One summer day my brother brought a king snake in to watch its useless efforts to move across the great room floor on the slippery tiles, much to our mother's fright.

It was an old house and Mom and Dad always planned to replace it with a new structure but that didn't happen until I had been married for a little over two years. It still stood between two giant valley oaks, and so was a landmark for people traveling along Highway 198 on their way to the Sierras. To preserve the ambiance, Dad had the house cut in half and moved to Farmersville –each half going to one of his Mexican foremen to be placed on their lots. The new house sitting on the original site is now seventy odd years old and was remodeled a bit after my sister-in-law and brother, Vince moved in and remodeled again when his son Russell and his family took over more recently. Alas, the two giant oaks have fallen and been removed.

We children so loved the old house we didn't think much about its foibles but my husband likes to tell the story of his first visit while dating me. He lived in a fairly new house (10-11 years old) in Redwood City so had no rural experience at all. He said, "It was the only place he ever stayed where the mice ran up and down inside the walls all night and all were served steak for breakfast!" Apparently, he was not discouraged by this.

Now my look back is over several decades (actually four score plus) but if anything, it is an even more loving look, as time has covered it in an abundance of happy memories.

Pare Down To The Essence

How often has the lure of makeup, music, high heels and fancy hairdos inflated my expectations—of on-going fun, of constant attention, of being transported by an out of body experience! When finally the evening is over, the thought that lingers is "All that glitters is not gold."

As much fun as it is to get dressed up for a special occasion, it is equally rewarding to pare down to jeans, a T-shirt and no shoes. "Child, what bare feet you have," says Mother Earth. "The better to feel your silky surface", I say.

Ever since God said, "Let the water under the sky be gathered into a single basin so that the dry land may appear" (Gen. 1:9), I have been fascinated by the dry land "God called earth." Like the primary colors, red, yellow and blue, there are three types of soil; sand, silt and clay and an unending assortment of mixtures of these three. Sand feels grainy to the feet, tends to let you sink up to your ankles and is usually light colored. Silt is dark and slimy when wet, like you are walking on silk material. Clay is different still—so thick that when it is dry it is like walking on boards but when wet it oozes between your toes and holds you fast leaving sunken footprints to dry so all can see where you trod. Some soils contain minerals; oil, gas, gold, copper, silver, sulfur and many I don't know. Working in the county assessor's office on a summer job, I came to know that people could buy and be taxed on the land, the personal property on it, and the minerals rights under it, making each piece of ground a different value.

But all this is too much information. Going barefoot is what I like: footraces in the dust, covering each other with sand at the beach and making models of country towns with water and red clay soil while sitting in the shade of the orange orchard on hot summer afternoons.

Somehow I don't think people are speaking of this scene when they refer to "being grounded," yet this childhood connection seems to have seeped into my pours through my feet. When I'm feeling disgruntled and off balance, just walking the beach or my garden in bare feet seems to restore my equilibrium. Leaving nothing between me and God's earth is a paring down to my basic connection. My stay here will be short when measured against all history but I have enjoyed thinking of all who have come before and felt this earth with their bare feet. It has held up well—this Holy Ground — may it last for the many bare feet yet to come.

Aunt Myra

Aunt Myra was an unassuming capable lady who figured prominently in my life but was never in the foreground at family gatherings. She wasn't actually my aunt just as the three Fitzgerald women weren't whom I also called "Aunt." In reality she was my great Aunt, the sister of Mom's mother. When Mom's mother died in an automobile accident when I was two or so, it seems she just took us on like a grandmother. She lived on a double lot in town next door to Mrs. Hader.

Aunt Myra and Uncle Will had no children but had adopted a son, Will Jr. He was just leaving home when I remember going to her house; he'd be two months away, then two weeks at home, never really holding onto employment very long. Mom said he'd been spoiled pretty badly. Their yard was exotic to me for even though we had cotton and alfalfa, peach trees as well as a family orchard of pears, apricots, apples, pomegranates, walnuts and almonds, we did not have figs, loquats or mulberries. When the fruit was ripe we were allowed to eat to our heart's content. She also had a snowball bush that I often thought should be planted right next to our lilac bush. The deep purple and snow white balls complemented each other so well.

To go on with the story, we usually went to Aunt Myra's after Mom had picked us up from the Catholic school in town as Mom either wanted to visit or we girls went for a fitting as she sewed for us a lot. If Mom wanted to visit, we'd always ask if we could go next door to Mrs. Hader's yard.

She was a widow who worked full time and her two daughters went to a caretaker after school. They had two of the best things in the whole world in their backyard—swings! We would hate to go home and leave those swings.

In her house Aunt Myra usually had a quilting frame set up with interesting work stretched on it. We could not touch it. All her tables and dresser were covered with crocheted doilies. Her house was one great room with windows on three sides. The kitchen sink was under the window by the front door on the north wall. A fireplace was on the west wall, a double bed sat in the southeast corner, a door to the bathroom in the east wall next to the cook stove and the quilting frame in the middle next to the kitchen table. On the bed was a beautiful crocheted bedspread that I was to have when she died or when I got married which ever came first. After her husband died and she got ill, she came to live with us for several months. She was always pleasant and grateful for any little thing Mother did for her. I don't remember when she died but I do remember asking for the bedspread and Mom saying Will Jr. and his wife had cleaned the house out before Mom got there. It wasn't the spread so much as the fact I would have just liked a memento of the aunt who was so talented and kind to me. She really was clever with her hands. When I was a baby, she had made a crib quilt of the sunbonnet girl. It wore out as it went through the family but I still have the one square with my name on it. I guess that is my memento!

The one event I particularly remember was being fitted for my confirmation dress. It was made of white dotted swiss organza in the princess style with a V neck and long fitted sleeves. It had to be hemmed and there was a discussion about the length; I wanted it at the knee and "they", Mom and Aunt Myra wanted it below the knee. Needless to say, it was finished below the knee. But that wasn't the biggest issue! In horror we all three realized the V neckline was much too low and since it was already finished to the lining there seemed to be no way to rectify the problem. We all sat there. Mom didn't want to hurt Aunt Myra's feelings but neither was she going to let me wear that dress, especially to church. Soon Aunt Myra picked up some scraps of lace and started to wind them in a circle. She said she could make a fake flower that could be attached to the base of the V and it would stand up high enough to cover any cleavage a twelve-year old might have. It was agreed and when we came to pick up the dress a week later, she had affixed the most beautiful ornament I had ever seen. None of the other girls would have a dress like this!

The summer I was eleven, before the dress incident, Aunt Myra came to cook the noon meal for the weeks of peach harvest. It was during World War II and pickers and help of any kind was hard to get. Dad had joined the "Bracero Program" and built a bunkhouse for several men to be housed in, maybe six or eight. Mother even helped in the field that summer. She and I stood at the grading table from six to four with breaks mid-morning and mid-afternoon and an hour at noon. The pickers poured their buckets of peaches on the table and we turned them over and over to be sure each was perfect before we rolled them off the end of the table into a 50-pound box. When the box was full, Dad or some other man lifted it off and on to a waiting trailer. Then my brother Vince would quickly put an empty one in its place. We wore long sleeved shirts buttoned at the neck and wrists to keep the peach fuzz from itching us. It was a worse irritant than the 100 plus degree heat. I wore a bandana on my head while Mom and Dad wore hats to keep the sun off their faces. I loved going out into the field straight from the breakfast table because the braceros would be there singing. Most of them spoke no English so the songs were in Spanish except for Mexicali Rose and Spanish Eyes which were the only two I knew. I could sing these two with them. I loved hearing the men sing. The orchard rang with their beautiful voices.

Dad conversed with them in sign language. He showed them just what color and size the peach should be when it was ready to be picked and pointed out the damaged ones—those with "brown rot"—those with a brown spot on the bottom of the peach. These should just be dropped on the ground. Somehow the Bracero Program brought the men food at noon and we would go to the house for lunch, actually a huge meal Aunt Myra had prepared.

At night she and Mom would put on another full hot meal while we bathed in hopes of cooling off and getting rid of the peach fuzz. Dad would still be gathering full boxes onto the trailer and bringing them out of the field so the cannery truck could pick them up for delivery to the cannery. The truck driver always brought a "swamper" to help transfer the boxes from our trailer to the truck. For some reason, these two men unloaded the trailer from one end causing the load to shift and fall into the dust in the yard. All of us who were in our pajamas ready for bed had to dress (well, Dad, Vince an I) and while Dad parked the car so the lights shone on the mess in the yard, we all picked up peaches and put them back into boxes for the two men, then bathed again and went to bed. Aunt Myra must have gone home each night because Mom stayed in the house with the younger ones. But Aunt Myra was there early the next morning to cook the noon meal and watch the two younger girls at the house.

The only other poignant memory of Aunt Myra was when I was in high School. My classes started a week or two later than the grammar school, so Mom and Dad decided to go on a week's vacation—the only one I can remember them taking before I left home at twenty. They had bought a new car and peach harvest was over so they were driving to

Portland, Oregon. To visit Mom's cousin and family. Aunt Myra and I would take care of things while they were gone. The folks had arranged transportation for those who were in grammar school. Aunt Myra had her model A Ford to get groceries or for emergencies. We had just gotten our first phone about a year before as well as the new car, so Mother felt more comfortable leaving. After all, now she could phone home to see how things were going.

On wash day, Friday I think, I was in the back bedroom stripping the rest of the beds and already had a load of wash going on the back porch. All of a sudden, I heard a blood-curdling scream. I ran the length of the house and out to the back porch where my brother, Patrick, had his arm caught in the wringer. Somehow, he'd turned it on and then tried to feed a piece of clothing through as he'd seen me do and in went his fingers then the whole arm and the wringer just kept going around and around at the shoulder. I slammed my fist down on the release and the wringer flew apart. We gently pulled his arm out and Aunt Myra arrived with a big towel to wrap it in. I carried him (about 4 plus years old) to her car and off she drove the five miles to the doctor's office to see if it was broken. I called the doctor's office to say they were coming and two and a half year old Betty (Elizabeth) and I sat on the back step for a long time. Betty had her salt shaker trying to put salt on a bird's tail because as the story goes, if one could do that one could catch a bird. I guess I was praying that Patrick would be OK. Finally, I went back to the chore of finishing the washing. When they got home Aunt Myra said that nothing was broken. He just had a bad rubber burn under his arm and the upper arm was badly bruised. Thank goodness!

We talked about it at dinner and agreed that all would be alright and so we would not tell Mom if she phoned, they would be back to Fresno to Dad's brother's tonight and home tomorrow. The phone rang. Vince sprang from the table and answered "hello." His next words were "Mom, Patrick got caught in the wringer and had to go to the doctor!" No matter what I said when I got the phone, they said they would be home in two hours. Boy, was Aunt Myra mad! She had not wanted them to cut their trip short. Besides Patrick was all bandaged and on the mend. It probably was the greatest trauma we had to deal with without the folks.

Chronologically the next memory of Aunt Myra was of the weeks or months she spent in bed at our house during her final illness. That part is all very fuzzy. She herself though, did have a clear and profound influence on my life.

A Five Year Old's Perspective

Clowns, black sheep and eccentrics—every family has them. Uncle Pete, whose real name was Moran Aloysius, was called "Buster" by his brothers and sisters. Pete (Peter) was the name he chose at Confirmation so we were instructed to call him Uncle Pete. He and his brother Larry, my dad's younger brothers, lived with us for a while as their father had died when they were young. His goal in life was to have fun or so it seemed. The stories of his high school years were all about crashing parties, stealing watermelons and turning outhouses upside down.

One summer night I begged Pete and Larry to take me to a party with them and their friends. I don't know why my folks let me go! I must have been five or six years old. The party was outside and all were gathered around a huge bonfire. As we sat around the fire eating hot dogs, a group of the guys suddenly decided to throw Uncle Pete into the fire. I'm sure he had pulled some practical joke on them and it was a good time to get even. Seeing what looked like grown men threatening my beloved Uncle Pete (he took me wherever I wanted to go) frightened me and I set up a howl that caused them to stop. Even though they had let him go, I continued to scream. Uncle Pete's punishment for his practical joke was to have to leave the party early to take me home.

Uncles Pete and Larry partied till they were well past the age of responsible adulthood. Uncle Pete did marry though, had four children and became a very good mechanic for Peterbilt Motors. I loved his laugh, his jokes and the fact he took me with him whenever he could. I even took my first boyfriend to visit him apparently for his approval.

Uncle Larry, sadly, really was the black sheep of my father's family. He borrowed Dad's clothes and partied so hard he would come home without the shoes or coat. It wasn't long before Dad put them both out of the house.

Uncle Larry drank excessively and in the end was in a terrible automobile accident while driving drunk. He was put in the hospital near the southern California border in an unconscious state. As time went on, he remained in a coma for two years. When my aunt, his sister, was asked how long she thought he would last, she said, "A long time since he spent most of his life pickled, he's well preserved!"

KNIGHTS OF THE OPEN ROAD—OUR ANGEL

Not much sticks in the mind of a five-year old but looking out the window on a fresh May morning and seeing a stranger sitting in the yard eating was something to remember. We lived on forty acres that my dad farmed five miles from the nearest town. Men did stop occasionally around midday and ask for food but never that early. There was the deaf mute that drove a Model-T and usually showed up at

Frank.

sunset. He was always surly and cross, no doubt a result of his extreme frustration. No one could understand him and few in the 1930s knew what a deaf mute was.

I was extremely curious about the man in the yard and was right there when he returned his plate to the back door. A short rather dark-skinned man with laughing brown eyes, he politely knocked on the screen doorframe, handed back the plate with an almost unintelligible "thank you" and headed toward the barn. As it turned out, this was the beginning of my first long lasting friendship.

It seems that Frank, as we came to call him, had actually come the night before and asked for food and a place to sleep. Dad had told him he could sleep in the barn as long as he did not smoke. The next morning, he told Dad he had to do some work in order to pay for the night's lodging. Since my folks had just begun purchasing these acres of old olive and prune trees, alfalfa and other pasture and had three small children, soon to be four, there was more than enough work to go around. One job and one day led to the next and soon Frank became a permanent fixture much to the delight of us children. Mom cooked for Frank also and as winter came on in 1937 he began to take his meals in the house and a permanent cot with sheets and blankets was arranged in the pump house.

Frank had a Sicilian accent that was no easier to understand as time went on but my brother Vince, who followed Frank everywhere he went, became fluent in the translation of his words. He was so fluent that when Mom or Dad needed to understand what he had said, they would call Vince. Frank didn't get paid much in cash. He got his room and board and clothes and as times got better, $5.00 monthly. Then he would walk to the country store and return with a giant bottle of root beer or 7-up both of which were foreign to us kids, a

Mom and Dad, me, Vince, Fran, Eileen, and Bill.

Me, Vince, Frank (in back), partial of Fran and Bill, Eileen in front.

large bag of salted peanuts and a package of Wrigley's Spearmint gum. I would set up my children's card table on the lawn, bring out a dish for the peanuts, five cheese spread glasses and we would have a party. When the drinks and peanuts were gone, we each got a piece of gum and there was one left for Frank as by then there were four of us (who could chew gum) and Frank. On Saturdays and Sundays, we loved being with Frank. He always had time for us and our parents were so busy!

Eventually we came to know Frank's story. He was Sicilian and from the time he was a teenager had dreamed of owning an olive orchard in California. It seems this place has long been envisioned as Paradise to people all over the world. He sailed from Sicily as a young man and on arriving in New York he managed to get a job with the railroad which was building lines to the west. During the '20s which was probably Frank's '30s or '40s he went to night school and studied for his citizenship while saving every penny he could. He allowed himself no luxuries and I suspect no time or money to socialize.

Finally, the day came when Frank gained his most precious possession, his citizenship papers. He withdrew all his money and hopped a freight train for California. Apparently, his natural amiability and his trust of others did not stand him in good stead. On his trip west Frank was accosted, his money and citizen papers taken and he was left for dead. Somehow, he managed to heal physically but he never recovered from the loss of his dream. He became one of the many homeless vagabonds who wandered the highways and byways begging for food and work in the 1930s. Frank did get to see much of the west and was working his way south through the San Joaquin Valley when he spotted the olive trees at the front of my folks' ranch. So many of these men stopped at our house, that Mom and Dad thought our house had been marked somehow as one of the places a "knight of the open road" could count on for a meal.

We had no tractor and Dad spent long patient hours trying to teach Frank to plow with a team of horses, but Frank was afraid of animals and would shout at them hysterically, which only spooked the horses and caused them to bolt. After one such incident near the yard where we were playing Dad decided Frank could hoe weeds, help clear the old prune orchard, irrigate the new walnut trees, burn brush, keep up the vegetable garden and cure the olives from the ten or so trees near the road. Frank didn't care what he did as long as it was honest work and kept him off the road. He also was a natural with whoever was the baby at the time. Often in the winter he would come in early and entertain the baby as we listened to the radio shows of the Lone Ranger, Tom Mix and Little Orphan Annie while Mom cooked dinner and Dad did the evening milking.

Frank's room was the pump house; a room about ten feet square. It had a cement floor, throw rug, window, door, cot, shelf and pegs to hang his clothes on, with the pump purring persistently in the corner. Frank had the usual toiletries on the shelf and a small mirror hung by the door. He always came to dinner washed, coifed and clean. This particular winter evening he'd put on a clean long-sleeved shirt under his bib overalls. We'd all said grace and passed the food around the table. Suddenly Frank grabbed his left shoulder with his right hand, then his left thigh with his left hand. A look of surprise came over his face and he seemed to be clutching something in each hand. We all stared. Frank excused himself and went to his room. Coming back shortly, he said, "Lizards better outside." We children thought he was very brave and very funny at the same time. Apparently they were hiding in his shirt and when it got warm in the house, the lizards started to move around.

Frank loved fruit pies and since we grew apricots, apples and peaches, we had lots of them. We established a day that we called Frank's birthday and Mom always made him a pie. He was so grateful! They are peculiar, these fragments of memory that come to me about Frank. I can still see him sitting under the oak tree eating his lunch. In the summer we kids would take our lunch out and join him.

It was one of those winter evenings when I was in the eighth grade that it happened. I was folding diapers piled high on the couch, Fran was setting the table in the kitchen where Mom was cooking. Frank was sitting on one of the straight-backed dining chairs listening to the radio as intently as the rest of us. Suddenly he let out a low groan and started to slip sideways from his chair. I ran to catch him yelling for Mom. She held him and sent me for a wet washcloth as he was drooling from the left side of his mouth. Vince was dispatched to the barn on the double to get Dad who was milking.

I don't remember any more of that evening. I know he never came back after Dad took him to town. Because he had no money and the folks had precious little, he was housed at what was called the Old Folks Home, a county hospital. Children were not allowed to visit and he never got well. Mom had tried several times when he was with us to contact his family in Sicily writing what he told her to as best she could understand, but the letters always came back. Wrong address. The folks paid for his burial but there were no services.

No memories come to me after the night he had his stroke and I wonder if he ever regained consciousness. How long did he live at the Old Folks Home? Did he miss us kids? Could he tell Mom and Dad good-bye without Vince to interpret? A great sadness envelopes me when I think of his life and his passing. Did he even know how much he meant to this group of barefoot children who were always welcome in his room? I guess it's not too late to say, "Thank you Frank for all the treats and more especially for the hours and hours of company and conversation-such as it was!" I do not remember you ever being cross or angry. I suspect that because you were missed that winter and the emptiness was never acknowledged, I still miss you to this day.

Frank's dream (like most of ours) played out differently than he had hoped; but he did arrive at a ranch that grew olives in California and had a family of very loving children who hung on his every Sicilian accented word. To us he was the angel who came in the night and stayed.

Emma Lindeman

Emma had a pleasant but nondescript face and hair fixed in a braid that wound across the top front of her head. I don't remember her saying much but she was Mom's shy, "spinster" friend always present at our rather chaotic holiday family functions. Her contribution was a green bean casserole that over the years, became the butt of many a joke, and sometimes a box of thin mints. My sisters recall that Dad and my Uncles Pete and George would tease her until they got her to laugh.

Emma worked for the Southern California Edison Co. and walked to and from work. Her home, situated across the street from St. Mary's Church on Church Street, was inherited from her parents. She had been adopted from a very large family, given up because the family felt they could not take care of one more child. She had no siblings and to quote my sister, "Mom felt Emma was very hurt by this and never wanted to get in touch with her real parents. In her later years she did eventually contact her siblings and they are the ones who took care of her and also received all her lovely antiques." I don't know how she and Mom met but suspect it was at church or as working women in their 20s. (Mom worked at the Tulare County Tax Collector's office for about ten years before she married.)

Emma was very proper and her clothes fit her demeanor. She knitted, and sewed blouses, skirts and dresses even a coat; no pants were worn by women in those days. Though she made every single piece, Emma's clothes were special and right in style. In those days after cutting an item from cloth using a paper pattern, the pieces were "basted" together—meaning hand sewn with long stitches, sometimes tried on, adjusted, then stitched on the machine. The basting held pieces in place and smooth making it easier to feed under the sewing machine foot. Though we had little cash and only one pair of shoes at a time we marveled at Emma's frugality. I sat many times and watched her carefully pull the basting thread out and wrap it around a small piece of cardboard to be used again and again. She also crocheted doilies for arm and head rests of upholstered chairs. One of my sisters says she also caned her own dining table chairs. Much to our delight Emma bought very few shoes so our brood was treated to her extra shoe coupons during WWII as our shoes were always either wearing out or being outgrown.

Emma was kind and generous to us but certainly not warm or affectionate. Because she lived across from our church, we (all eight of us) occasionally spent parts of Sundays at her house usually two at a time. The five of us girls all spent some time singing in the choir and our three brothers each passed a time serving mass. On holidays, or Holy Days, we sometimes sang at two masses and the boys served at another so in between we went to Emma's for breakfast, to change clothes or to wait for our ride home which included bringing Emma home to dinner. We sat and watched her sew listening to classical music coming from her record player or from the beautiful radio console. She seemed to like our company but there was nothing personal about it. Her availability to us must have stretched over some twenty years.

One sister says she remembers Emma asking Mom to save the water she'd boiled string beans in so she could take it home to

Emma, me, and Dad.

make soup. We all can recall the holiday Dad stood between Mom and Emma and putting his arms around each, gave them a joint hug breaking one of Emma's ribs. Poor Dad was embarrassed and apologetic and got a lot of teasing from the other adults.

Mom loved music so when I entered high school, and there was a piano teacher across the street, Mom arranged for a noon lesson I could walk to. The only reason this worked is because Emma gave us her piano. Sadly, the recital at the end of the school year fell on the same evening as the spring dance. As soon as my part was over (not done very well) I was out the door and back across the street to the dance. My sister Dorothy later fulfilled Mom's wish for a piano player. Ten or fifteen years later when my husband and I had a place for it, my three brothers brought the piano to our house in Watsonville. This was for my husband to play as I never became proficient. I was so glad to have it as I loved to hear him play. We kept this huge upright until1967 when we traded it in on a new more appropriate sized piano. Hearing piano still reminds me of Emma.

The younger girls remember her house as a fascinating place made up of perfectly restored antiques set about to be admired but not really used.

Elizabeth remembers all the smaller pieces had a number on the bottom, which fed into a catalog she kept. She was promised Emma's silverware when she married but that did not happen.

We all remember her telling with pride of her trip to Europe and of having an audience with the then Pope. Dorothy remembers Mom buying Emma a gift each Christmas and the both of them enjoying each other's company during long visits after many dinners. I'm sure she was an important link to the work world in town that Mom so missed living out on the farm with only one car. Eileen remembers that Mom was Emma's Power of Attorney, and

when they were in their early 70s and Mom was diagnosed with Alzheimer's disease, Emma quickly found someone to drive her out to the ranch to get the key to her safe deposit box. I remember all the ration coupons she graciously gave us during WWII—not only for shoes but for sugar, coffee and pepper—three essentials of life at our house.

Emma, like Frank, was actually another member of the "village" that helped raise us children, being generous and supportive and all the while expanding our horizons.

Emma, Mom, and Catherine.

You Can't Go Back

Hot dusty roads, temperatures exceeding 100 degrees.
Rivers that run through the ranch in summer—
  blackberry vines up the sides.
Hide and seek, foot races or softball from dinner to dark.

Learning to swim after Dad finishes milking; we sit in the shade of the orchard and wait. One at a time he takes us into the "ditch" (as we call the big Tulare). He tells us to kick our feet and shows us how to move our arms. He takes us into the water after stripping to his shorts. When we had adjusted to the cold water off the Sierras, he throws us several yards up stream. If we do not yet know how to swim the current carries us back to him. Back to sitting under the tree as Dad takes my brother, Vince, then my sister, Fran, and finally my youngest brother, Bill. Evening after evening we delight in having Dad's whole attention and learning something new.

A few years later we could go alone up stream to a stand of big oaks where grapevines as big around as a quarter hung down to the ground. The neighbor boy, Vince, Fran and I in mid-afternoon trucked through the hot brown dust to our special spot. There we took turns grabbing one of the vines, backing away from the ditch bank as far as it would reach, then running toward the ditch, flying out over the water, letting go at just the right moment and dropping into the deliciously cold water. This particular spot may have been five or six feet deep. As we came up for air, the current was already carrying us downstream to the place along the bank devoid of berry bushes and less steep where we could climb out— only to run back upstream to do it again.

That ditch held hours of fun for me. In late July the water level usually dropped considerably as farmers all along the line took out their share to irrigate their orchards. Then Dad would put one of the peach picking ladders in the water so we could climb up to get whatever berries the birds had left.

Gradually the water slowed to a trickle, then just a few deep puddles. This was when we caught catfish and pollywogs trapped in the water holes. These we carried to the house to put in the wash trays to watch. The hired man, Frank loved to eat the catfish and when wash day came, we had to dispose of the pollywogs even though they had not yet completely turned into frogs.

In the fall, after school had started while the days were still warm the dry sand of the ditch was a perfect place to do my reading assignments and dream. It was such a peaceful place without little brothers and sisters and chores.

How quickly those oaks and vines disappeared—all gone now but then that was seventy years ago. How time flies!

Nature

"October gave a party, the leaves by hundreds came -
The Chestnut, Oak and Maple and leaves of every name"

Third grade—Friday afternoon—recitation time. Each week we
had to memorize parts of a poem. This was an anxious time, yet
one of some excitement. Poems brought mind pictures and to
be able to memorize fascinated me. We had not yet approached
the drudgery of having to learn our times tables by heart and so I
immersed myself happily in word pictures.

"The gingham dog and the Calico cat, side by side, on the table sat.
'Twas half past twelve and what do you think, neither one
nor t'other had slept a wink."

I could see the stuffed animals in my mind though not at all like
our real ones.

Regardless of how much I liked school and of how the poetry
could put me into any season or time, I dearly loved staying
outside. My damaged skin, currently rejuvenating itself, is proof
positive that while growing up we spent every possible day all day
outside! It was the sun and moon and the growing things, not so
much the animals that spoke to me.

The first memory after moving to the ranch at about four and a half is of the Easter I awakened and looked out at the tall alfalfa growing across the driveway. There was a rhythmic pattern of depressed spots in the wind-blown field of alfalfa equally spaced across the big expanse. The Easter Bunny must have hopped right across our field to get to our house!

In years following this same area was planted to peach trees— yellow clings that Dad sold to the cannery. It was the blossoms— their fragrance and delicate construction that captivated me in the spring time. Years later while I maintained a household in Salinas (row crops, no trees) John had a crop loss case in Visalia. It involved a peach orchard from which John brought me a picture of a healthy blossoming peach tree that I had framed and kept on my desk for years. It immediately called to mind the beauty and exact fragrance I'd experienced wandering the orchard each spring.

On another part of the ranch Dad planted walnut trees. They are precious and beautiful in a very different way. Growing 20'-30' wide and 30'-40' high, they are great to climb and their shade was/ is invaluable in the hot sun of the San Joaquin valley. They do not have blossoms but are deciduous like peaches so when the new green leaves come and the nuts begin to form in their Kelly green hulls they are majestic. In the fall, after the pickers had harvested all the nuts, they were run through a huller and then dried on large trays. Now they are dried in a dehydrator, like a giant clothes dryer, then stored and sold in 50 lb. gunny sacks. After the pickers had left, around Thanksgiving, we children, dragging a large gunny sack took to scouring the orchard looking for any nuts that had been missed or had dropped later. This was called 'gleaning' and we earned our Christmas money by collecting as many pounds as we could. There was a cost though because in picking up the nuts and removing the loosened hull our hand turned a dark brown so, even after soaking our hands in lemon juice each night, everyone at school knew you were working in the field. The one Christmas I remember, made it all worthwhile because a new Sears Roebuck catalog had come. I spent many evenings studying it and carefully selecting a Christmas gift for each of my five younger siblings. I still remember the thrill when my order came, and I secreted myself away to gift wrap each piece.

The other way to earn spending money—also outdoors—was to have Mom sew a strap on a gunny sack which each of us (my brother and I) dragged through the cotton field at the back of the ranch. Picking cotton hurt your fingers as the bolls that had been such pretty pink and yellow flowers earlier were now dry and rough. Cotton weighed so little, it took days to get the sack full. I was happy to graduate to the job of writing down the weight of each picker's sack before he dumped it into the cotton trailer to go to the gin. The best fun was jumping into the high mounds of cotton again and again. The November weather was cold and foggy. The cotton was warm in the after school hours when the fog had burned off. Then on Saturdays, having progressed in math, I was set to work adding each man's pounds picked that week and multiplying by two cents. Occasionally, during those seventh and eighth grade years, I even made out the checks for my dad to sign. I guess because there were no neighbors or telephones, I looked at these jobs as fun and as a challenge. Sitting idly or folding diapers was certainly no fun. Only now do I see how thoroughly and deeply I was being taught responsibility.

Indian summer was one of the best reasons for living on a ranch. Starting school in September meant enduring the last really hot spell of weather. Since we went to school in town five miles away, this meant a long sweaty ride home in a uniform meant for winter. My thirst was unquenchable and my ego somewhat deflated as this school was so much more demanding than Deep Creek. A few weeks into the school year, Dad had cleared the watermelon patch in order to prepare the field for fall panting. When we got home, going through the garage to the house to change clothes, we saw a pile of watermelon as tall as I was and about six to eight feet wide. These melons were 12-18 inches long and were stacked on the cement floor—all that was left of the old pump house. Without even asking, we knew our after- school snack was watermelon. We rushed to put on play clothes and then pick out the biggest melon. Mom said one a day so we took turns picking out the one for the day, then dropping it on the cement to crack it open. The one whose turn it was, got the heart –all of it! The rest of us broke off pieces of the juicy thirst-quenching fruit. When there was nothing left but the rind, we were a sticky pink mess! Did we care? Certainly not! All the troubles of the day and most of the heat evaporated eating our fill of watermelon, sitting in the shade of the umbrella tree in the back yard. And so September passed, one melon a day.

LEFT: At Elizabeth's baptism. Fran,
Elizabeth, me (holding her),
Dorothy and Eileen.

Years later, back row—Fran, Elizabeth, me.
Front row—Eileen and Dorothy.

My 8th grade graduation, 1945. (Me, front row, far right)

CHAPTER THREE

THE FORTIES

In late October 1944, I became a godmother to Elizabeth, my baby sister, which made me feel very grown-up. I don't think I was very attentive to her through the years. I married at twenty-two and started my own family soon after. Lots of special events happened in the mid-to late forties that I'd like to mention. In late November-early December '44 Frank had his stroke and left a big hole in our family. Then in June 1945 I graduated from eighth grade and that summer was a live-in babysitter for the Hipwell children. I finished that babysitting job and went to L.A. with a cousin of the folks. Her husband was a dentist in the Navy and since she and her two young sons were alone, I suppose she took me along for company for a week after visiting my folks. On August 15th, the whole world celebrated VJ Day. I remember the horns, bells, shouting and sirens waking me from a nap that Sunday afternoon. We all got in the car and went to a drive-in for a coke. It was packed!

When Visalia High School started in September my whole life changed. I rode the bus to and from school every day and with no phone at the ranch plans were never altered and there was no staying after school for sports or Girl Scouts. I really felt left out! At the end of my sophomore year

Dad sat me down for a talk. An insurance policy the folks had taken out on me matured on my sixteenth birthday so I had a choice to make. I could continue at Visalia High and graduate, go four years at San Jose State to get my teaching credential (I still was determined to be a teacher) OR I could transfer to Immaculate Heart High School for girls in Hollywood where one of my eighth-grade girl friends had gone in 9th grade as a boarder, then I would have to attend the junior college in Visalia and only go two years to San Jose State. I was up for an adventure! Hollywood here I come! This time the bus rides were on the Greyhound Bus Line. I was familiar with the line from summers working at the court house. I got there and home via the Orange Belt line, a subsidiary of Greyhound.

There were two of us girls from Visalia, two from Hanford and two from Delano. We loved it when we got the Burma Shave driver as he was called—The Burma Shave Co. put up billboards with limericks on them every few miles of highway. These would remind our driver of a popular song and since we had all been in choirs for years and knew all the popular songs, we sang for the whole four-hour long ride. No idea what other passengers thought but in '47-'48, and '48-'49 there were still lots of service men traveling the bus lines. All joined in!

Academically I again went from being head of the class in Latin II, to nearly flunking Latin III. Living on campus did have its pluses; sports every day after school—no tennis—but volleyball and basketball; then trips to Hollywood and Vine every weekend to see the latest movies and movie stars, listen to the newest records, attend countless radio shows as audience along with all the service men on leave. We walked Sunset and went to Grauman's Chinese Walk of Fame. Some Saturdays were spent at Griffith Park and the Observatory not far from the school at the corner of Los Feliz Blvd. and Western Avenue. The school had thirty to forty boarders living on the west wing of the second floor of the convent with about the same number of nuns living in the east wing. The first year I slept in the dorm with seven other girls and my senior year I had a room with a junior, Clare Tona from Lancaster. We are still friends. We valley girls connected with Connie Castruccio and Elinor Biaggini, from Laguna Beach and Cayucos. Margaret "Fitz" and I formed the four from class of '49. We all four attended the reunion of '09 and Margaret and I went to gatherings in 2013 and 2019.The boarder's section of the high school and the college are gone but there are still movie stars enrolled in the Jr. High and High School. Lots of changes in the landscape.

Connie, Elinor, Margaret Fitzgerald and I became a foursome who spent lots of time together even after our graduation in1949 and had our own reunion in March of 2013 in Cayucos, California. Some stories from those two years are included. We all agreed these years at the Catholic high school were the most influential of our lives.

My Favorite Teacher

Who was my favorite teacher growing up—now that's hard to say. Since there was no such thing as kindergarten when I was growing up, I was a full six years old when I finally got to go to school. Two seventh grade girls walked me the quarter mile down the road (now highway 198) to the two room eight grade school called Deep Creek School. There were about 30 in our room and my teacher's name was Miss Trapp, or was it Miss Devine? Anyway, between my second and third grade she married and became Mrs. Trapp or maybe Mrs. Devine.

I was so glad to be there, I was bored staying home with my three siblings on the ranch every day, I would do anything to please, and so quickly became the teacher's pet. After I finished my work, I was allowed to make copies of worksheets using the tray of gelatinous material on which an ink stencil had been placed. I could work quietly making 10 to 20 copies on newsprint in the back of the classroom watching Miss Trapp teach. This ink stencil on a gelatin material was probably the first xerox machine.

The hygiene standards at school were not as stringent as ours at home so I missed half of the school days with several childhood diseases. At Christmas the teacher came to the house with the full set of Dick and Jane books for me to study during the Christmas break. Still I passed, though only provisionally. What most impressed me about first grade was

Sister Paula with the 4th grade class.

that in January and February the farmers in the area took turns bringing a lug (40 or 50 lb.) box of oranges to school for the morning recess. Everyone got one and was thrilled as I'm sure several had had no breakfast. I loved my teacher of these first three years as she was always kind and made school fun! I wanted to grow up to be just like her.

After breaking my right arm the summer, I turned nine, September finally came and school was about to begin. Only this time my brother, Vince was coming with me and we were not going to Deep Creek School. We would be attending the parochial school in town five miles away. This was a much bigger school with only two grades per room. My cast was removed and school began but alas I could no longer write with my right hand, not legibly anyway, so I had to use my left. Every night I had to practice my penmanship beside homework which I had never had before. It didn't take long to realize that I also was really behind the other students. What was that funny half box the teacher drew in math?

Division was totally foreign and I had never heard of times tables. There was always time to play after school. While waiting for the car pool, and for the upper grades to get out, I decided to give the jungle gym bars a try. Without thinking about the muscles that had been weakened from being in a cast, I swung out, lost my grip and landed on my left wrist. Even I knew it was broken; another six to eight weeks in a cast!

Now my handwriting was illegible with either hand. Poor Sr. Paula! Between being so far behind in math and not being able to write my homework legibly, I was getting depressed. I'd gone from teacher's pet at Deep Creek to the bottom of the fourth-grade class. I also developed a stuttering problem which Sr. Paula cured me of by imitating me. When I heard her stutter, it sounded so bad, I quit immediately. About a month into fourth grade Sr. Paula made an announcement to the class. At the end of the year she would give $1.00 to the student who improved the most. In the fall of 1940 $1.00 seemed a huge amount.

Besides the bribe, I remember Sr. Paula for the athlete she was. When baseball season came, I was in heaven and both arms worked. We played every recess, noon and night after supper on the ranch till dark. Sr. could really hit the ball and watching her run the bases in her full-length habit with the beads swinging from her waist made her one of us; not the teacher, not a nun. I was so enamored of her that both my parents and the other nuns began to think I would become a teaching nun. But my goal was to win the $1.00 and I did! Being around Sr. Paula confirmed my desire to be a teacher as I saw that one could be the teacher and still play baseball with the kids.

The number of good teachers I had did not stop at fourth grade. My fifth–grade teacher, whose name I can't remember, also left me with a lasting impression, this time more serious. Midyear, my cousin, Edward, who was in the fourth grade was accidently run over and killed. Since the school was adjacent to the church when it came time for the funeral, the whole school lined the walk on both sides as an Honor Guard. The casket passed between the lines. Edward was one of five boys and my favorite. We played together frequently, usually Kick the Can in our orchard while our folks played cards. It was just so sad to think I would never see him again. On going back to class, I could not stop crying, let alone concentrate in class. Sr. gave the class an assignment and took me outside to visit. She asked about me and my favorite subjects. Of course, I told her baseball. She listened and gently helped me move on. This teacher taught me that I and my feelings mattered. She did tease me about taking over class if she were ever absent as I tried hard to always know what was going on in both grades.

My eighth-grade teacher taught me a different lesson—that other peoples' feelings also mattered. In May we were to have the annual crowning of Mary during the May procession. There were only four girls in our class and nine boys. The privilege of crowning Mary went to a girl and all wanted the job. Sr. Alphonsus called three of us into a meeting one noon hour. She reiterated the awards that would be handed out at graduation and confirmed that each of us would get one. We already suspected what they were and also knew that quiet shy Madeline was not in line for any of them. Sr. said, "Since each of you will be getting an award in a few weeks, wouldn't it be nice if we four agreed to ask Madeline to crown the Blessed Mother this May?" We all agreed since we were each happy with our awards. Sr. then called Madeline in and told her we all agreed that she should crown the Blessed Mother this May. She was beaming! I don't think she knew or cared she wasn't getting an award this graduation. This way of telling her also affected me. Now I felt empowered. Sr. could just as well have left all of us out of the discussion and appointed Madeline to the job. The way in which she handled the issue made a big impression on me. The benefits of sharing were far greater than the advantages of accumulating as many awards for myself as possible---and I was competitive! This way of handling people and problems seemed to dovetail nicely with the discipline I received at home. The influence of all these teachers and my parents led me to a very confident young adulthood.

St. Patrick's Day—1945

Coming of age is indicated in many ways but basically means being able to face the world as your own person. Usually this giant step is the result of having passed certain tests, i.e. the driving test or graduation from a certain grade level. It can also be denoted by physical changes such as voice changes and facial hair in boys and breast development and the commencing of the menstrual cycle in girls.

In years past there were many more ways of telling if one has come of age, so to speak. Were you responsible for carrying out tasks assigned to you? Could you accept the consequences of your actions and decisions? All of these imaginary lines needed to be crossed and re-crossed. When we are growing up we can be responsible one day and not the next, be a good care-taker for an hour or two but no longer; even work all day when the task is a new challenge and totally flake out when it is the third day in a row of a menial task.

For girls and boys, the meaning of coming of age is so different. Hers may depend on the first time she gets to wear makeup or go on a date and for him it may be when he gets to take the car out alone or gets his first beer. There are plenty of times of experimentation so it is really hard to say when one actually comes of age. Perhaps only in looking back can one determine when we really came of age, or at least when we think we came of age. For me the day that I thought I had finally arrived was a certain St. Patrick's Day.

Dad belonged to a fraternal order called the Knights of Columbus and Mom belonged to the Catholic Daughters, in fact it was at one of their joint activities that they met. The two groups had lots of socials together and also did charitable works for the community together. Every St. Patrick's they held a dinner dance to which anyone could come by just paying the admission charge. Whole families came as long as the children were eighth grade or older. Most of the women if not all, wore corsages and were very nicely dressed and the men all wore ties and coats.

St. Patrick's Day.

Since September I had been taking ballroom dancing with a lot of other eighth and ninth graders. These lessons had culminated in a winter ball. I was so excited. I went with Lloyd and my dress was black velvet to the floor with a round scoop neckline edged in white lace. There was a black velvet drawstring that ran through the lace and tied in a bow at the front. Mom even took me to a photographer for a portrait. This dance was much more fun than I anticipated and made the lessons all worthwhile. It even wiped out the memory (mostly) of the night Dad ran out of gas while bringing me home from my dance lesson. We had to walk the last two miles home in the cool night air. I was exhausted and never gave a thought to Dad who had to walk back with a can of gas to get the car. My first Winter Ball certainly was a special event but not as memorable as the St. Patrick's Dance the following March.

Somehow the fact that it was spring colored the whole evening. It just seemed magical, maybe because of its uniqueness. It was probably the only time I got to go out at night with Mom and Dad by myself. I remember the corsage; it was a camellia that had no scent and therefore suited me much better than the gardenia I got for the Winter Ball. Mom had one too. Both came from her friend, Catherine Toomey's house. She grew them in her hot house and had made the corsages. She was also my godmother so gifts from her were not unusual.

The band played during dinner but as soon as the dessert was served, the first dance was announced. It was for fathers and daughters, mothers and sons. Being able to dance with Dad just seemed to be the highlight of my life up to that point. I don't remember the thought process, just the feeling that if I was good enough for Dad to dance with, I was good enough to face the world!

CHILDHOOD VACATIONS

Living in the great San Joaquin Valley meant we could see the Sierras but not the Pacific Ocean or any other ocean for that matter. Being able to see the mountains enticed us to want to climb their heights when we went on a vacation. Not being able to see the ocean really motivated us to want to go see it, touch it, swim in it, fish in it and do whatever else one did there. Thus, on the only two occasions (in my memory), when Dad decided he could take a week off in the summer, we children debated for days about where we should go—to the mountains or the ocean? Who knows how much input we really had, but we argued and planned as though we were the sole planners of the trip.

The summer I was eight Mom and Dad rented a cabin in Sequoia National Park. They had two families with whom they were really close who owned cabins there. We had driven up for a Sunday meal at one of these cabins or the other several times. There were five of us children now and Eileen was only one. On one day of that week, Mom's sister and family came for the

Vacation in Wilsonia.

day. I probably wouldn't remember except I have pictures of all of us in my scrapbook. Mostly I remember the coolness and the smell of pines and redwoods, and the tremendous appetite we had after playing hide and seek in the trees for hours. We also played a game where one laid in a hammock and two swung it while another waved a pine or cedar branch above your nose. You had to keep your eyes closed and imagine you were flying. One really did get the feeling of floating free.

It was during one of our hide and seek games that I found out how hard redwood trees are! If you could get in and tag the tree that was "home base" while the person who was "it" was out looking for you, then you would be free and not have to be "it." I saw my chance and started running toward the home base tree not realizing that I was running down hill—a very steep hill. There was just no way to stop and one leg rushed past the other in giant out of control steps. Just past the tree was the road into the park. I don't know if I was afraid of cars or just could not have altered my course if I had tried, but I hit that tree head on. I did turn my face sideways and the bark of the tree nearly removed all of the skin from my cheek. I landed in a heap with no breath to yell, "Olly, olly oxen free!"

All in all, we had a great vacation especially because we slept so well in the cool mountain air. Over the years, Vince and I spent a week or two, he with the Toomey boys and me with my friend Margaret at the Fitzgerald's cabin—her aunt and uncle's. They took us on picnics and to campfires at night. Some days Margaret and I spent hours reading Nancy Drew books and the Ave Maria magazine. Other days Aunt Pat or Aunt Eileen would fix us huge lunches to take on long hikes. We were a group of six or eight if the Cutler boys joined us.

There was a huge meadow across from the Fitzgerald cabin filled with wild flowers. I can still see the buttercups, poppies, lupin, larkspur and

Queen Anne's lace gently waving in the breeze. Sometimes just Margaret and I would sit on a stump and eat our lunch, then pick a few flowers to press. One summer we decided to make a birthday card for Aunt Ann with the pressed flowers. Margaret attached the flowers, wrote a poem inside and drew a picture on the front. Then she wanted me to sign the card but I was furious because I hadn't been able to contribute so I ran away and hid; sulking for two—three hours. Poor Aunt Pat nearly had a heart attack looking for me. Being able to do one's part was a requirement at our house, so I was very frustrated at not finding a way to do my part. (Margaret, an only child, didn't get my reaction). Aunt Pat very kindly told me everyone has different gifts and though mine were not artistic, I was gifted in other ways. That evening I was allowed to hand the card to Aunt Ann and sing her a song. In the valley Aunt Pat was always our babysitter when the folks needed one so she knew me pretty well. What a dear diplomat Aunt Pat was.

Finally, those who wanted an ocean vacation won! The summer I was fifteen the folks rented two cabins side by side in the resort town of Cayucos. They were right at the shore along with six or eight others. Mom and Dad and the three youngest were in one and the five oldest were sleeping in the other. Both had kitchens and we had breakfast and lunch in the cabins. My sister, Fran and

Vacation at Cayucos.

I had brought bottles of Johnson's baby oil which we mixed with some vinegar in hopes of getting a sun tan.

Me with my first fish.

One of the first days Dad rented a rowboat and took Vince and me fishing. Vince caught a huge fish about twelve or fourteen inches long and so did I. When I reeled mine in, I got so excited I just screamed with joy. There were several row boats on the water in the cove and of course all looked our way. I think Dad was pretty embarrassed. When I got back to work at the Court House the next week one of the ladies said, "You sounded pretty excited about catching that fish." I asked how she knew I caught a fish. It seems she and her husband were in one of the other row boats. She said, "Sound really carries over water and she'd recognize my voice anywhere." Then I was embarrassed!

The day after our fishing expedition, Fran and I tried out our suntan concoction. Here at the coast the sun didn't come out till between ten and eleven but after breakfast and a walk through town we couldn't wait any longer. Besides it was already warm though still foggy. We had books to read and made ourselves comfortable in the sand on towels. Fran quickly tired of reading and was up and running after our brothers or doing something else. I must have laid out an hour on each side. Little did I know that sun through fog at 80 degrees is much more devastating than the bright sun of 103 degrees at home. After a half day in the row boat (though Mom had insisted I wear a hat and shirt over my bathing suit), and lying on the beach for two hours I was a beautiful crab-like color and I could hardly move. My skin felt much too small for me.

The next day Dad had tickets to go out early in the morning on a big fishing boat. For some reason, Mom had planned to stay at the cabins with the three youngest while Dad took the five oldest out. She suggested I stay at the cabins and she would go with Dad. I gladly played games with Dorothy, Patrick and Elizabeth (Betty) and fixed their lunches. I also followed Mom's strict instructions to keep sunscreen on them and myself at all times. I took their pictures with my Brownie box camera and generally enjoyed the day. Thanks for trading places, Mom.

The sunburn was the worst part of that vacation but going out to dinner every night for six nights was the best part—NO DISHES! Years later I was to get another sunburn that made this one seem minor.

Pat and Betty (Elizabeth).

Eileen and Dorothy.

Beginning High School—Visalia

Going from a class of thirteen to a class of 250 is quite a jump. Riding the bus was another big change. Since the kids from my first three grades at Deep Creek were also on the bus it wasn't a bad experience. I remembered two families who picked up with me again though we hadn't seen much of each for the five intervening years. John and Arvin Fly and Gertrude and Victor Lewis were great to me. John and Gertrude were an item, plus John could drive And, he played on the basketball team. Great advantages!

Of the four girls in my grammar school class, one, Margaret Mary had gone off to the Catholic boarding school in Hollywood. Another, Madeline seldom came to high school as her father thought she was more valuable working at home. She was the oldest of eight as was I. Thank goodness, my folks felt strongly about education for both boys and girls. That left Shirley and me and we lived on opposite sides of town but we did

Me, 1947.

Shirley Heller.

see each other at church. Having no phone meant all weekend plans had to be made at church or school or on the bus.

It was easy to pick up with the old group from Deep Creek since Arvin and I had been first graders together so now as freshmen we sometimes got to tag along with John and Gertrude. Mr. and Mrs. Fly would include me going to basketball games. In the winter in the San Joaquin Valley tule fog was a real hazard. One night going to Modesto on highway 99 was particularly foggy. Mr. Fly drove very slowly and one of us hung out the window watching for the white line and another watched for the telephone poles on the other side to help him stay in the lane. The drive was definitely a team effort.

Somehow freshman year was a little like first grade. I got a very bad case of pleurisy (which recently the doctors have confused with pneumonia) and then the mumps; one of the childhood diseases I'd missed in grammar school, as had my dad. Unfortunately, I gave them to him and my seven siblings. I missed a lot of school but, with the help of Dick Cutler — one of the boys who had been in my eighth grade, I passed. He would bring my algebra homework to the house and spend time explaining it to me. His mother was a schoolteacher who substituted at the grammar school. She drove him out to the ranch and also helped me.

In English class, we had to write book reports and the Cutlers even picked out books for me from the library. The ones I remember that made a big impression on me were the biographies. *Jane Addams of Hull House* was about a social worker who started neighborhood centers in Chicago for the poor inner-city immigrants. She also lobbied to pass just work laws regarding women and children's hours and was instrumental in setting up the first Juvenile Court. From her I acquired an acute sense of justice particularly where women were concerned. The other biography was of

Sr. Elizabeth Ann Seton, a wife and mother who converted to Catholicism and as a young widow organized the first parochial school in the United States. She also started the Sisters of Charity, a teaching order of nuns which she headed until the end of her life. She really appealed to me as I had felt intuitively that I wanted to be a teacher since the fourth grade.

Also, during this year Shirley and several other girls and myself walked to our grammar school convent once a month for religion classes after school. In sophomore year this evolved into a coed group called the Neumann Club that met at night and had social activities. My folks would take me into town for the meeting and then one of the older boys would drive me home. This was exciting as we lived five miles from town and there were always guys who wanted to go for a drive; sort of a date before I could date. The tacit belief was that anything connected with "church" was OK. Not so! As I was to understand even more thoroughly years later. Even or especially, church functions and laws need to be evaluated objectively.

In my sophomore year, we had a gym teacher who taught us calisthenics for 45 minutes daily five days a week for about five months. Some girls hated it but I loved it and felt healthier and more in shape than ever before or after! In the spring, we had tennis which was new to me and seemed exactly my "cup of tea!" I was elected to be the Commissioner of Tennis for the next year for the GAA, (Girls Athletic Association). This turned out to be a road not taken as I transferred to the Catholic boarding school in Hollywood to join Margaret Mary the next year instead.

Immaculate Heart High School.

MEMORIES OF IMMACULATE HEART HIGH SCHOOL

It was a warm Saturday afternoon in the fall of 1947. The Sisters had decided to take the boarders who stayed weekends on a wiener roast and picnic to Griffith Park in the Hollywood hills. After dinner while it was still light about 6 pm several of us, seven or eight, asked to go hiking. "Fine, as long as you are back before dark. We want to be back at school by dark."

Off we went. We chose a trail that went slightly up from the picnic grounds. All talking and climbing we paid no attention to the distance we'd gone. As it started to get dark and the trail got steeper and steeper we realized we could no longer see or hear the picnic grounds and the trail had become so steep it seemed wiser to continue up rather than to go down and risk falling, though we knew we would catch heck for being late. We began to see glimpses of head lights above us so we continued. After much struggling through brush and helping each other up (the trail seemed to have disappeared) we found ourselves on the street in front of the Griffith Observatory. It now was DARK! The observatory had just closed so there was no using their phone. We discovered a pay phone in the parking lot, but what to use for money?

Penny loafers were very popular in the fall of '47 and being IHHS girls we had DIMES in each shoe. I was chosen to use one dime and phone Sr. Nepomucen at the convent to ask what to do and to let her know we were all right. She was the principal and much feared by most. I hesitantly dialed the number and found she was ecstatic to hear from us. She told us to walk downhill on whatever street we were on to Franklin St. and catch the streetcar to the front of the school. "Did we have any more money?" We all looked at our shoes and counted the dimes. The ride cost a dime and there were enough for each of us to ride and one or two dimes left over. We were instructed to come right up to the front door, not to walk up Los Feliz Blvd. and around to the back entry where students usually arrived.

Now we had only to walk from the observatory to the Franklin St. streetcar. There were street lights but they were few and far between. We all started out bravely and even started singing when suddenly we became aware of a man shouting at us and chasing us. The street was steep and one of the girls tripped and fell, yelling "Wait, wait"! I think I yelled "Stop." We all did and started back to pick up Phyllis. By then the man had stopped and was laughing his head off at having scared us so badly. We regrouped wondering why we had run after all there were several of us and only one of him. We waited a short time for the streetcar and finally arrived back at IHHS.

Walking up the grand driveway to the front door and into the exquisite parlor was a time stopping moment for me. This farm girl had never seen such luxury even when dressed in my best and here we were all dirty and scratched, tear-stained and relieved to be back. Relieved was not the word for the look on Sr. Nepomucen's face. We were welcomed with open arms!

⋊⋌⋪

In 1947-'48 most orders of nuns were not allowed to drive. Still IHHS had 2 or 3 cars. I had transferred into the school from Visalia High School that fall as a junior. I had obtained my driver's license that previous summer learning on my parents '39 Ford. I had driven mostly on country roads and in a small town of 13,000. Early in October (I think) I was called to the office and asked if I had a license to drive. My friend Elinor was also called in. We were told that two nuns needed a ride to the Pasadena train station every Friday to catch a 1 pm train. We would be allowed to be late to our class after lunch.

The next day was Friday and we were to report to the garage after our lunch to meet two nuns and get the car. I was to drive and Elinor was to direct me as she had been in L.A. area since her freshman year and knew the city much better than I did.

First, the car was a Dodge and the starter was on the floor under the accelerator, not like the Ford. Second, we were to enter noontime traffic making a left turn uphill onto Los Feliz Blvd. Third, no one told us the nuns would be reciting the rosary rather loudly and constantly all the way to the train station. We got out onto the street without incident but by the time we reached the top of the hill thick black smoke was pouring out of the back of the car and it smelled like something was burning. Elinor suggested I take off the emergency brake. Whew! That helped, but the nuns were already starting the second decade of the rosary and it was hard to hear Elinor giving me directions about which lane to be in, in order to turn left or right and when. Country roads only had one lane in each direction.

Somehow our guardian angels were with us and we delivered the nuns to the train and made it back to school safely and with no scrapes on the car. This continued till Christmas vacation. Although I got better at driving in traffic and we had memorized the route to the train station, the nuns never stopped saying the rosary.

MEMORIES FROM THE FALL OF 1947—WHY I WRITE

I like to tell stories! I like to make people laugh!

My sisters and I always say, "In our family we laughed when we should have been serious because the serious was too hard to bear." It would have brought us to a place too low to get up from—never mind that we sometimes laughed till we fell on the floor! Laughter, like tears, is cleansing if it is true; hollow laughter is a bitter form of ridicule and should be banished.

I remember my first trip home from boarding my junior year of high school. The oldest of us, probably we five, we're still at the kitchen table long after nine p.m. when our house usually was required to go silent. I was regaling them with stories—the adventures of the young and foolish Valley Girls in Hollywood. How we helped one another get our rooms ready to pass inspection as early as possible on Saturdays so we could go downtown. There we looked for movie stars while we window shopped or ran from one theatre to the next between the early show and the second show, then ran to catch the bus to get in the door by the six-p.m. dinner bell. Sometimes we had a milkshake at the shop on the corner of Hollywood and Vine, spent hours trying on hats in the hat shops, or listened to the latest records in the booths supplied by the shops at the time. The bright lights and celebrities walking down Vine Street were terribly exciting to a farm girl who didn't even have a phone at home. We laughed that night with the kitchen light on way past ten. I was the star of the show and so glad to be with my brothers and sisters again. I'd been gone almost three months. We sat at the kitchen table with the one overhead light while the folks went to bed as did the three younger siblings. I felt very grown up — a bit apart — yet encased in a cocoon of family so rich and welcoming it is a wonder I could return to school after that Thanksgiving holiday!

><><><

One of my last encounters with Sr. Nepomucen was a meeting about the last week of school. Sr. had a habit of interviewing seniors she thought might have a vocation to the convent. This idea had never entered my head so when she asked me what I was going to do with my life, I said I was going to go to college to become a teacher. "Yes", she said, "but what are you going to do with your life?"

In my thinking, I had only progressed as far as getting a credential and a job teaching so I nonchalantly said, "I guess sometime I may get married." She responded rather disdainfully, "Anyone can get married." Knowing how hard my folks worked to keep it together, I got angry and snapped at her, "Not everyone can stay married!" "You're excused." She said quietly. Years later my sister told me the nuns were so convinced I would join them that they had told my dad he would get the two years tuition back if I joined the convent. Since I usually tried to please my dad, I'm very grateful I didn't know that at the time. Needless to say, the insurance policy didn't quite cover the bill!

THE CONTINUOUS LIFE

I have fleeting glimpses of a cherished childhood made so by hardworking, optimistic, faith based parents. One of riding my tricycle on the huge porch singing to the full moon a song I had concocted of words I'd gleaned by listening to adults who mostly listened. Is the performance more important than the audience, or vice-versa?

Then the competition, foot racing, broad jumping, high jumping all conducted during the long twilight summer evenings with the "big" Indian boy, Marshalino, who came to "play" after a long day's work in the fields and always won, then stood and grinned as we, my brothers, sisters and I, tried harder and harder. Where did he come from? Where did he go?

Another glimpse is seven to ten of us playing Hide and Seek and Kick the Can well after ten pm in the pitch dark peach orchard with only the light ablaze in the house to nurture our sense of safety. Our parents were playing cards alternately laughing then seriously discussing the events of the early days of WWII.

Memories of my ten-year-old self standing daily from 7 to 4 at the peach-grading table are framed by the melodic singing of the Braceros whose harmonizing seemed to materialize from within the foliage of the fruit trees.

The war ends and all changed. I turn thirteen and take my first of many summer jobs—babysitting all summer for four cousins under eight years old. The hot summer weather was miserable, but was a gift of sun and stars after the cold tule fog winters.

One last powerful glimpse is of a New Year's Eve babysitting my seven siblings, plus the three Toomey boys and the two Peltzer children with no phone and five miles from town. I remember baby Elizabeth waking for her 10 o'clock feeding after all had been put to sleep except the oldest Toomey boy, David. I went to change and retrieve Elizabeth; I drew a bottle of formula from the fridge and ran hot water in a pan saying to David "heat the milk and I'll be right back." When I returned to the kitchen he had poured the bottle of milk into the water. I laughed at his lack of knowledge and retrieved another bottle of formula and showed him how to let it sit in a pan of hot water till it was room temperature. Thank goodness Mom had left extras.

It is the feelings I wonder at — complacency, joy, contentment, being safe and secure, confident, bored, curious, and always with the thought, "tomorrow will be an improvement over today." How did my parents emit these feelings to us? Was it with actions, words, smiles, touch (not so much), food, warm house, care for others was always evident, fairness, music, song, dance, eating three meals a day together for years, tears and laughter? Or did these feelings come from living with siblings whom, in those days I could not get far enough away from but can't get close enough to now? I know no way to find out. The Dalai Lama says, "If we think we are something special or not special enough, then fear, nervousness, stress and anxiety arise. We are the same." "It does help quite a lot to see your-self as part of a greater whole." This may be the underlying teaching my parents lived. Connection to the family brings joy while isolation breeds sorrow whether we are speaking of the nuclear family or of the larger group — humanity.

Writing Memoirs - How She Made Me Feel

I guess I like writing memoirs whether or not they are meaningful to the next generation. They gladden my heart, like Sunday, when granddaughter Justine, said her dad was taking her out for a driving lesson in his old pickup that required learning the stick-shift method. I was immediately thrown back to being her age, seventeen, and a boarder at the Catholic high school in Hollywood. I had been elected to drive the principal, Sr. Nepomasen, to graduation rehearsal. It would be held at a public place in the Hollywood Hills. In the late '40s the nuns were not allowed to drive, but they had a car or cars given them. This was a Dodge; we had always driven Fords on the ranch. Yes, I learned to drive in the peach and walnut orchards where the trees did not move and you had a good chance of not hitting anything. I had driven this car in the Hollywood traffic before so no problem getting to our destination or parking.

After rehearsal on coming back to the car, I saw we are parked facing up hill in an area that was very steep. In this car, the starter is on the floor near the accelerator, as are the clutch and the brake. I could start the car while parked, but what next, as I only had two feet. I instructed the Principal to put her foot on the brake and keep it there till I told her to lift it. We manage to get off the hill without incident, killing the engine, or hitting anything. Only later did I realize I had given explicit instructions to a lady almost four times my age, that everyone else totally feared! She took "no lip" from anyone and was known for her gruffness but this day she was meek as a lamb and showed she could take orders as well as give them.

In these moments alone in the car in downtown Hollywood with the Principal, I forgot her gruff voice, her rigid rules, and felt totally empowered by her ability to transfer her authority to a lowly seventeen-year old senior from the farm.

High School Graduation, 1949.

CHAPTER FOUR

THE FIFTIES

The fifties were again full of change; I like change apparently! Lots happened in these ten years. More than I could possibly foresee.

The agreement was I would come home, go to the Junior College in Visalia, and then transfer to San Jose State. Agreed, but as Margaret Mary got ready to return to Hollywood to Immaculate Heart College, I felt a wisp of nostalgia. Her dad was giving her the old car and she was going alone to take all she needed and herself to her dorm room. Since her school started a week before my classes I offered to ride with her, help her unload and go visit my aunt in Sant Monica for the weekend. I'd take the bus back home.

Margaret arrived later than expected to pick me up and was still fuming because after she had packed the car her dad made her totally unpack it and do it over, making sure heavier items were on the floor. She'd had them up in the back window and he'd said, "If you stop short, they'll hit the driver in the back of the head." The route over the ridge from Bakersfield to L.A. was called highway 99 at the time (now I-5) and we were having a great visit. Just as we crested the ridge near Lebec, a driver coming north suddenly crossed over crashing into us and throwing me into the front passenger corner of the car (no seat belts in 1949). I developed a black eye, a bump on the head and a terrible head ache but otherwise no one was hurt. The other driver was on something and didn't know where he was. We were stranded! Waiting for the Highway Police and trying to figure out what to do seemed like forever. Luckily, it was not five minutes when the family from Delano (a year behind us and still in high school) came along headed to Immaculate Heart High School. Mr. Zaninovich stopped and somehow got us and our bare essentials into his car and on we went. I remember taking the street car from IHHS to Santa Monica to my aunt's and putting the wrong change in the bus pot. The driver started to correct me, looked at my black eye and said, "That's OK." I had headaches for a few weeks but no permanent repercussions. To this day I do not put anything on the back seat or window that is heavy and Margaret Mary is glad she repacked her car.

The first year of Junior College (College of the Sequoias) was mostly fun — going to school with boys and beginning to date, majoring in education and sports and singing in the Spring Musical. Mom and I again hung up the wash singing all the songs to *The Desert Song* freshman year and *New Moon* sophomore year.

The second year of junior college was equally exciting. I had been elected head of the Associated Women Students so served on the student council. That year Fran was Senior class president in high school and Mom was Grand Regent of the Catholic Daughters. Dad joked he had to address three women in his house as "Madam President" before he could speak.

Upon graduation from College of the Sequoias, I again went to work for the summer at the courthouse. My boy-friend's sister, Mary Lou, worked in the same office and early in August asked me to go on a weekend trip with her to Santa Ana. Her Mom had relatives there and wanted to visit them but had arthritis so bad she could not drive. We arrived late Friday night, leaving after work, and on Saturday while

Mom, sixth from the left, at Grand Regent meeting.

Mrs. Kirby visited, Mary Lou and I decided to go to the beach. It was a very hot day and after lathering ourselves with tanning lotion we found a vacant beach and stretched out about 11:00 am. After working all week and the long drive from Visalia the night before we soon fell asleep. I had on a two-piece bathing suit, which I seldom wore; apparently we slept for quite awhile. When we woke, I knew I had gotten the sunburn of my life! We high-tailed it back to Mary Lou's aunt's house, showered and put on cream.

The next day I was so red everyone was worried and appalled. This time, not only did my skin feel too small; it was too small. I could not stand up straight as my midriff really hurt. It had not been burned this badly ever. Sunday afternoon we started our drive home over the ridge route. Mary Lou was driving, I was sitting in the front passenger seat and her mom was sitting across the back seat in a pile of pillows. I was turned around talking to Mrs. Kirby when BAM! … we hit another car. It had pulled in front of us making a left turn into Gorman, a little settlement with a restaurant about three hundred yards off the highway. Before I knew what had happened, I had gone through the windshield and come back through to rest in my seat (still no seat belts in 1951). Mary Lou seemed stunned and her mom had slid off the back seat onto the floor. I reached over and turned off the car. Somewhere in the back of my head I'd heard that you do this so the car won't catch on fire. I told Mary Lou I'd walk to the restaurant and call the highway patrol. As I got out of the car, I saw the other driver walking drunkenly in circles, then urinating on his car. I started off, probably taking a few steps when I started to faint. The last thing I remember seeing was a man in a beautiful white shirt coming towards me. Though I felt terrible about it, I couldn't stop myself from falling into his arms. The next thing I remember I was on a stretcher in an ambulance and so was Mrs. Kirby. Mary Lou was sitting with us. I asked for my rosary and she went back for my purse. I wanted to apologize to the man with the white shirt but he was gone. We headed for the hospital in Newhall. When we got there Mary Lou called her aunt and uncle in Santa Ana and they came right away.

Mrs. Kirby was taken to x-ray and the doctor told me he would have to stitch my cuts; one was within a quarter inch of my left eye and the other was under my chin. He said the job was all the more difficult because he couldn't tell my skin from the blood because I was so sunburned. Of course, he was kidding! The male nurse had me hold his hand while the doctor administered the Novocain to deaden the area and afterwards feared his hand would never be the same. After I was all stitched up, Mary Lou's uncle wheeled my bed over to the pay phone and I called home. It was just dinner time and Dad had finished milking. I asked him to come get me and Mary Lou and to let Mr. Kirby know he needed to bring an ambulance for his wife as the x-ray showed she had a broken hip. Dad said he'd pick us up in a couple of hours. Now I knew it was at least a three or four-hour drive so I said, "I want you to come get us, not join us" He laughed and said he would bring my sister Fran along to keep him awake. Fran did talk a lot! I guess Dad had warned Fran about what she might see as I had told him about the stitches in my face but not about the sunburn. So, Fran seemed prepared, but Dad was pretty upset when he saw my sunburn. He said, "How old will you be before you realize the sun is not your friend?" Dad and Fran had arrived at the Newhall hospital about midnight; we loaded up and started home. After taking Mary Lou home we got to the ranch just in time for Dad to do the morning milking. The sunburn made me nauseous and I was exhausted from the trauma, besides I looked awful so I missed a week of work. By the time I went back it was almost time to get the stitches out but not quite and my sunburn had started to peel. Everyone at work asked what the other guy looked like and generally teased me. I must have looked pretty bad because the evening of the day I got the stitches out Dad came to my room and offered to take me to see a plastic surgeon if I wanted. The doctor had told me to apply olive oil frequently every day and the scars would fade. I thanked Dad and said I would follow doctor's orders and stay out of the sun.

Scars do fade, but the memories of how they arrived do not.

At birth our bodies are so perfect, precious to behold. Then the challenges of our lives begin to unfold. Should we strive to die a completely untainted vessel, or is the goal to survive the scars with which we wrestle? These are questions for the philosophers of our times but I suspect it's not the bodily marks that matter as much as whether we continue to act out our lives with humor, persistence and wonder.

By September my face was sufficiently healed and I was off to San Jose State.

CHILDHOOD MEMORIES OF WATER; CHRISTMAS BREAK 1949-1950

The rains—how they came that fall! It seemed they never stopped and so no work could be done in the orchards, especially no pruning. It had been a good year crop wise and the harvest of peaches and walnuts was done. All eight of us were on break for two weeks and able to help Mom with whatever she needed so Dad decided to take a much longed-for trip back to his roots in Goodhue, Minnesota. This was the place from which Grandpa Hutcheson had migrated. Selling his one-fourth of a section of land, he moved his young family—his wife, two sons and a daughter to sunny California. My dad was just 6 or 7 and the oldest of the family when they left Minnesota but he fondly remembered his early childhood friends, the O'Reillys, and some cousins, as many had come to California to visit through the years, though he hadn't been able to go back.

Dad left the day after Christmas. The rains did not let up. It rained and rained and in listening to the radio, such as it was, we older ones secured bags for sand and felt a flood was eminent. Two rivers ran through our property, from east to west. Our ranch was located about 40 miles west of the base of the Sierra Nevada Mountain Range between the newly built Highway 198 that bordered on the south and the larger of the rivers. Dad had just finished planting a brand new peach orchard. Fearing the young trees would die of too much water, we five oldest were up at dawn, down to the river, filling bags and stacking them along the river bank. We could see the river had crested at the very top and were working feverishly where the bank was weak. Then we heard the neighbor from across the road yelling at us and looking back he was waving his arms frantically trying to tell us to get to higher ground as the river had already broken its banks upstream from our property and was filling in the young orchard behind us. We were in danger of being cut off from the house. We abandoned our work, grabbed our shovels and remaining bags, and rushed back home.

Later in the afternoon, Dad's younger brother, Uncle Pete who lived in Fresno, waded to the house leaving his car on the highway, and one by one carried us all to his car taking us into town out of the water's way.

About ten years ago we had a family reunion and in talking about this event, my sister, Eileen, swore I had not been present but I had remembered it vividly. Finally, our younger sister, Elizabeth produced proof positive with a picture of Uncle Pete carrying me and our brother Vince carrying her (Eileen) to higher ground through the flood waters.

The orchard survived and Dad returned after his week in Minnesota. All's well that ends well! The moral of the story is: No two people remember the same event the same way!

Christmas, 1949, the day before Dad went to Minnesota.

Me with Uncle Pete, Vince with Eileen, Christmas 1949.

"I write out of my inconsistencies. I write with the colors of memory. I write as a witness to what I have seen. I write as witness to what I imagine."

—Terry Tempest Williams

About fifteen years ago I started to write and stopped after a year for no remembered reason. A year ago I started again and found that stories I write now about the same subjects as prior stories, are different! Has my memory changed—added or subtracted to the events I recall? Why I really write is to capture a thought or happening that the family might find entertaining in times to come. I want to leave some stories, mostly true, that bring laughter and a little clarity to the events of my life as I lived it. I can imagine eyes lit up and grinning faces as they read some of these pages. Some weren't funny when they took place but now cause a slight ripple of laughter or a huge guffaw depending on how long ago it was and what actually occurred.

Like the time friends of our family came to get peaches and the oldest boy refused to help us pick them for his family. After we finished he was anxious to play a game of tag, and didn't see the cotton scales with its big hook for attaching one's bag of cotton hanging from the walnut tree in the front yard. As he ran under it, he caught his nostril on the hook and flipped himself backward to the ground. We gasped knowing he was hurt, but then smirked. After they left with the box of peaches we'd picked for them, we saw the whole incident as retributive justice, we roared with laughter … and talked about it for years.

Sometimes I just "write to remember." Like the time in my sophomore year of junior college when I had been elected President of the Associated Women Students so served on the Student Council. Some of us decided to organize a ditch day for all the P.E. majors and minors. There were about fifteen of us, called the PEDS. Rose, whom I'd know since fourth grade, and I would get our dad's pickups on a day when all of us had just one or no academic classes, those were usually M–W–F so we chose a Thursday in May. We knew the one or two girls could easily makeup their one academic class from that day, all our other classes on T–TH were physical education courses; this semester learning rules and regulations of individual sports like golf, archery, bowling, badminton and tennis. Rose and I would park our pickup trucks across the street at Merle's Drive-In about 8:30 a.m. As the other girls arrived on buses from Lindsay, Exeter, Tulare, Avenal, Hanford and Lemoore they would come over and join us, lunch and swimming gear in hand. We brought blankets, softball equipment and picked out a wide spot on the Kaweah River called McKay's Point for our "playday." Earlier that day, my dad and I had churned a gallon of homemade ice cream which he carefully packed in fresh ice for us. I had that in front with me. All the girls arrived and we got to the river about 9:30 on a perfect spring day.

After a totally relaxing May day of fun and food, jokes and jaunts through and along the river we gathered our toys and belongings and piled back into the pickups. Rose and I drove the 10 or 15 miles back to Merle's and arrived just as the string of yellow buses collected in the curved driveway in front of the College of Sequoias. We all entered the drive-in, some to the rest rooms others ordering cokes, then just before the bus drivers closed their doors the girls shuttled back across the street and jumped on board their respective buses. No problem!

The next day buses and class times arrived as usual. After greeting each other and other friends in the arcade we made our way to first period—I did get some suspicious looks, but was still so elated thinking we got away with our fun filled "ditch day" it never occurred to me to really look in the mirror. Needless to say, in mid-May in Visalia in 1951 sun screen was not high on anybody's list and everyone of us with particularly fair skin had faces that shone like large red apples. In those days the girls wore sundresses to school so our arms and legs were also an angry red glow.

Midway through first class, I was summoned to the Dean of Women's office and given the third degree. "Where were you yesterday? Were all the P.E. majors and minors with you?" I was still so elated remembering the fun, I told her exactly how we'd spent the day. My sunburn would have given me away anyway! "Why?" she asked. "For the sheer fun of it" I replied. "Are you sure there was no other reason? Why Thursday?" "Did I realize that Miss Bond," our instructor, "had absolutely no one in her classes and that she drove to all the parks she knew of in Tulare County looking for us before she finally left for the rest of the day?" I could honestly answer no. We never even thought of her all day as we were having such a good time. Once the Dean was convinced there was no malice aforethought, I was told we were each to apologize to Miss Bond. Then I was excused.

On looking back, I realize none of us liked her very much as she seemed to be such a grouch all the time, so maybe subconsciously the day was about more than having a fun "ditch day." All of us apologized and our sunburns eventually peeled off. In remembering, I now see that experience as a rite of passage. At almost 19 I felt I had successfully hosted my first adult social event. I guess we knew there might be consequences for flaunting the system but one fun day of spring rebellion was worth it then and still. The adults involved took it for what it was and were not heavy handed. Now I'm wondering if Dad and the Dean weren't a bit jealous wishing they could have had a "ditch day" too.

The Cedar Chest

Christmas of '51—home from college—much to do, tired. We older ones were going to midnight mass on Christmas Eve. Dinner was over by seven pm and we didn't have to leave till 11:15 pm. I decided to nap and going into my parents' room in the dark, I collapsed on their bed. It was the closest bedroom to the great room.

My parents came to wake me when it was time to go; apparently, they had been looking for me and were very surprised and concerned that I chose their room in which to nap.

"Why would she go in here?"

"Do you think she saw it?"

When I hear them talking; I awake and still in the dark, we three exit the room.

The next morning when I came out into the great room on Christmas morning there under the Christmas tree is a beautiful though plain cedar chest with a card with my name on it. I know now it was being kept in their room as a surprise having been delivered several days before I got home from San Jose State. What to say? I didn't want it—didn't need it—didn't ever intend to marry, so why collect things that indicated I might. It was a Lane Cedar Chest, beautiful, bulky and unbelievably heavy EMPTY!

I'm sure we moved it to the room that I shared with my sister, Fran. I was a junior at San Jose State that '51-'52 school year. The Christmas before, my then boy-friend had voluntarily joined the army which I thought was very stupid and was in Korea. His action further convinced me never to marry--men!

Cedar chests have auspicious beginnings. It is said that originally a chest was carved from a single solid block and they were first used by the ancient Egyptians to protect their golden treasures and to keep important papyrus documents from decay and insects. During the Renaissance they went from being one piece to several panels and some had drawers. They were used by families to come to America and again used by whole families to homestead the west. Later some were made with only a cedar lining to protect against moths. The Lane Company of Altavista, Virginia. (1912–2001) became the most popular maker of these chests in the U. S. They had been very proficient at making ammunition boxes during WWI and afterward turned their production-line to making Hope Chests. Shirley Temple was the star of their advertising campaign targeting GIs and absentee sweethearts of WW II.

But back to mine. I got married in mid-'54 and we moved several times (8) before settling in Salinas in 1968. I honestly have no recollection of where the chest was or when I rescued it from my parents' home until that year. It is currently still in good condition and in our bedroom. Tonight, I opened it and took stock. There are the usual keepsakes plus my tattered copy of the children's book, *A Hole Is To Dig*. Like the pharaohs I have my "gold"—a collection of silver dollars (that's another story) and a few coin collector's series. There are also a group of Mother's Day cards—homemade of course, prayer books, white gloves—girls, women's, my husband's M P gloves and arm band, my wedding dress, our square dancing outfits I made as well as a long paisley Christmas skirt with a matching tie for John I'd also made. But of all the things in the chest the one to bring tears is the to-from from Mom and Dad that Christmas of 1951. "I hope you like it" she writes, " Love, Mom and Dad" I see now it was really the cedar chest Mom had wished for and would have liked for herself.

A PIANO

Funny how in looking back one can see how different objects play either significant or insignificant roles in our lives — and what do I mean by significant?

As a child of two I lost my grandmother, on my mother's side, who died in a car accident. She, like my father's mother was named Margaret — thus my name, as the eldest grandchild, is Margaret. Margaret Chambers nee Fitzmaurice was by training a piano teacher at least until the invention of the tractor, at which point my grandfather, a blacksmith, lost his business and his beautiful two-story brick home in Kansas. He had to pack up his wife, his three daughters and son and immigrate to California in their four-seater car; the only asset he salvaged. Their oldest daughter, Aunt Gertrude, having already finished "normal" school had secured a teaching job and remained behind.

Landing eventually on Garden Street in Visalia where Grandpa got "odd" jobs, welding and occasionally shoeing horses for farmers who could not yet afford a tractor. They never again could afford a piano. Things seemed to go from bad to worse for several years. My mom was 15 and enrolled in school, as were her sisters and older brother. Upon graduation, Mom got a job at the local Court House Tax Collector's office. From graduation at 17 till she married at 27, Mom was to be the family's main wage earner. She paid for her brother's burial, he died of consumption, and for her two younger sisters' weddings but Mom never forgot her music. During these years she sang and danced in the local Community Theater every year. After we children came along, my mom's spinster friend, Emma, who had a piano but didn't know how to play, gave hers to us. During my freshman year of high school, one noon hour a week, I walked across the street from the high school to the piano teacher's house for a lesson. Finally, June came and so did the piano recital. Sadly, it was on the same night as the Frosh-Soph dance. I rushed through my pieces which I didn't know very well anyway, so I could get to the dance. I thought that ended any involvement with piano for me.

Fast forward to my junior year in college when I transferred from the junior college in Visalia to San Jose State. I had been dating a fellow at junior college who had joined the army (the Korean War) mid-sophomore year. At San Jose State I met another young man who pursued me relentlessly and who also happened to play piano. During free periods we would go into the auditorium where he played the piano for me for hours on end. Mid senior year he was drafted. I continued to date him and correspond with Bob who had already gone to Korea. Finally, in desperation I begged my parents to come to San Jose for a weekend as I needed to talk to someone (Mom) about which of these men to choose. As I described each of their attributes, I mentioned that Ed played the piano. That was all my mom needed to hear. "With someone who plays piano, you'll always have music in your life…," she said. And so, I chose!

After my younger sisters, who did play the piano, left home Mom gave us Emma's old piano for my husband to play. My three brothers delivered it to our house in Watsonville from Visalia in their pickup in summer of 1956. My husband did play and entertain me and the children. Nine years later we moved our six children to Fresno and my folks could visit more easily and also hear Ed play.

On a given weekend Ed's parents planned a visit from the Bay area. With the move from the coast to the valley, I found we had a few extra dollars and could trade in the now very old piano for a new one. It came on a Saturday late afternoon and Ed played it for his mother and dad. While his dad had been away for five years during WWII, Ed had played for his mother every morning before school and she dearly loved to hear him play. The weekend was a huge success.

We moved back to Salinas, the children took lessons on it and Ed played a few times, Christmas, etc. until the early nineties when he inexplicably gave it up entirely. Since then the physical piano became a source of contention. I continued to sing in a choir as I had done annually since I was nine (except for a few years when I was too busy) and I had so hoped he'd play. This fall getting ready to lay new carpet in the living room, we made the decision to get rid of the piano and much to my surprise I could not give it away! It seems there was a glut of pianos on the market. Having put flyers all around stating FREE PIANO, come and get it, nothing happened. Then my cleaning lady said if you are giving the piano away, my sister's boy is very talented but has no piano and is learning on a very small keyboard. We arranged a pickup day and she got a crew to take it away by 11:00 on a Saturday. What surprised me was my physical reaction. I got up sick that morning and had severe diarrhea till after the piano left. I knew it was to be used for a good cause and my living room is much more spacious, so what's my problem? I no longer sing, due to some throat issues, so I had no need for accompaniment. The cleaning lady has since sent me text videos of her nephew playing the piano and he is indeed gifted. Happy landings, piano!

THE SEVENTH STREET APARTMENT(S) SAN JOSE

Alice Keene Whitaker

Justine, Lena and I moved in together (all from College of the Sequoias) in September. Justine was older, had suffered Polio so one arm was useless, but she could do more with one arm than I could with two — like separate the white from yolk of an egg. We had one bedroom (twin beds) and a pull-out couch. We rotated every week. We also rotated the cooking and grocery shopping. None of us had a car and the biggest pain was carrying my dirty laundry to a near-by laundromat and back. That first year was all about learning time management and how to say "No" to guys.

John-Ed, me, Alice Keene and Ron Whitaker, 1951.

During this year ('51-'52) I met Alice in my education classes and the next year she and I and her sister, Marge, a nutritionist at the local hospital, roomed together in the same set of apartments. Alice and I became fast friends and still communicate. That senior year I learned a Manhattan was not just part of New York City and never forgot. Also, that year Alice met Ron and Ed and I, who had met early my junior year on an unasked for blind date set up by the girl next door, became an item. Ed surprised me with an engagement ring on New Year's Eve, and was drafted in January 1953. Ron joined the navy just prior to that. Alice and I graduated in June 1953 with our BAs in Education and our Elementary teaching credentials. Dad desperately wanted me to come to Visalia to teach but salaries were better in Santa Clara County and besides I didn't want to move home. Alice got a job in the Saratoga district and

Alice and me.

John-Ed, me, Alice and Ron, 1983.

112

San Tomas School in Campbell, my first class, 4th grade, 1954.

GRADE 4
CLASS
OF 1954

I signed on at San Tomas School in Campbell. I got a summer job in San Jose as Ed was stationed near-by. At the end of summer, I went home for a visit and was thrilled when Dad took me to a used car dealer and put a down payment on a '49 Ford sedan for me. Alice and I rented a one-bedroom apartment upstairs in a huge old home in Los Gatos and took turns with the car; she drove one week, dropping me off and I drove the next, dropping her in Saratoga. We never had an argument I can remember and at the end of our first year teaching we each married, me June 26th and she in mid-August. We attended each other's weddings-mine in Visalia and hers

at the Episcopal church at Lake Tahoe, (her dad was a Minister). Alice was a primary grade teacher and I taught intermediate grades. Her primary printing was flawless and she did a great job of writing JUST MARRIED on both sides and the back of my green car with white shoe polish. Being in love Ed and I thought it looked great, so left it on driving over Pacheco Pass in 110 degree weather midday on our way to Boulder Creek where Ed had

My wedding photo, June 26, 1954.

rented a cabin for our honeymoon week. Needless to say, the shoe polish washed off at the service station but left the car indelibly marked. Most of the time we ignored it, we couldn't afford to have the car repainted, but when a picture of Terri (4.5) and Joan (3.5) hanging out the window above those words appeared in the Watsonville Register-Pajaronian, we were a bit embarrassed.

When I met my husband on that blind date, he introduced himself as Ed Marcroft so that is how my family came to know him. As he was drafted and entered the work world, he was addressed by his first name, John, which his family and mine never used. His parents did not want him confused with his dad, John. So, in this writing and throughout my life I alternate calling him Ed or John, whichever comes out or whoever we are with at the moment.

Alice and I each had a baby girl the next summer. She and Ron lived in Cupertino while Ed and I took the Los Gatos apartment and I went back to teaching at San Tomas. Ed had six months of Army left and six months of San Jose State to finish. He graduated June 22, 1955, Cathy was born June 25th and our first anniversary was June 26th! Little did I know this was the way our lives would escalate for the next twenty years. In the next year Alice and Ron moved north and we each had another child; she another girl and us a boy. From then on, we communicated intermittently as they moved to the state of Washington. More children followed for both of us, unfortunately, our children never got to know each other. Neither of us ever taught fulltime again though both of us were active in community affairs and have basically been stay at home moms. As couples in the nineties, we spent a few weekends together. Their winter home—away from Yakima—has been in Borrego Springs and we had a delightful visit there one early spring. Ron has now passed away and Alice lives with one of her daughters, Sari in Idaho, Heidi in Belleview or visiting Wendy in Yakima. Her sisters, Marge and Marilyn have also passed away as have my sisters Fran and Dorothy and my brother Bill but we still have our health and can outwalk a lot of people our age. No doubt friendships like ours have helped us age well.

'55-Early '60s—Watsonville Years

With Cathy's birth in June, 1955 change took on a different meaning, from changing diapers to changing addresses. We were not supposed to have babies in our 49 College Ave. apartment so as soon as Ed got his job at Cal Spray Chemical in early September, we moved to a two-bedroom duplex in Campbell. With Ed taking my car to work and no stroller, life was pretty confining for Cathy and me. My brother Bill spent a weekend or two with us as he was at Santa Clara University and my brother Vince came for an over-night. My cousin, Johnny, was in an iron lung in San Jose at that time and his wife also visited. Their whole situation was so sad as Johnny was really an adventurous type but tuberculosis plus polio shortened his life. As teen-agers when he found I'd never seen the Golden Gate Bridge, he and I drove from Visalia and back one afternoon/evening up to and over the bridge and back just so I could see it. All lit up that night it was beautiful!

Soon Ed was transferred to Watsonville and given a company car to drive. Much better! After living in a duplex in Watsonville for a few months we moved out Freedom Boulevard on the edge of an apple orchard—red delicious! Michael arrived in August, 1956 the first SUNNY summer day we'd had. The summer fog of the coast had a depressing effect on me and took several years to adjust to after being raised in the San Joaquin Valley. I joined The Jr. Chamber of Commerce as Ed enjoyed watching the kids at night and I got to know a nice group of young people. We were chosen as a family to model in their fashion show. All fun!

Easter, 1955.

Then before long I was expecting Terri in the spring and we got serious about getting a house of our own. We found a lot in a new subdivision on the south side of town near the golf course. It cost $3000. We put $300 down and started paying $30/mo. In the mean time we qualified for an FHA loan. Terri was born May 3, 1958 and later that month, I signed a teaching contract at Salsipuedes School to teach a fourth and fifth grade combination. I withdrew my retirement from Campbell school district and we paid off the lot. Later in the fall, we started to build our own three-bedroom two bath house! We were so excited though shortly after I signed the contract, I found I was pregnant with Joan. It was a tough year for the three kids, but I was high on teaching and on the prospect of getting our own home. Easter vacation was the week before Easter and we had moved in about March 24th. Joan was born on Easter Monday, April 6, 1959 and I had been able to teach right up to the break. New neighbors, new friends, no more Jr. Chamber meetings. A gal from Moss Landing and I carpooled to a preschool in Watsonville that next fall, which was the start of great new friendships and five years of stability which we all needed. Cathy chose to stay home with Joan and me, while Mike and Terri couldn't wait to go to school. Since none of the families in the preschool had grandparents handy several of us started a babysitting co-op, which worked like a charm. Some of the same group got into square dancing later and then kept tabs on each other when anyone moved out of the area. We partied together, planned progressive dinners, swapped maternity dresses and got to know each other's kids as well as our own.

I had enjoyed living in the midst of the Red Delicious apple orchard but as I look back, our Guardian Angels must have been doing double duty. The house was on a busy road, Freedom Blvd. and had no fence. The Christmas Cathy was 18 months. She thought the red ornament on the tree was an apple and bit into it, causing her mouth to be full of glass. Scary! Then most mornings when I was pregnant with Terri, Cathy, Mike and I would go out after breakfast to tell Ed goodbye, and I'd watch the kids play awhile before I started any chores. One morning after Ed left. I rushed back inside to go to the bathroom, being eight months pregnant, when suddenly I heard horns-lots of them! Running outside, I saw Cathy but no Mike! Cutting through the orchard to the busy Freedom Blvd., I came on traffic stopped in both directions and a little boy marching along the white line with a white plastic bowl on his head, which he often wore as a helmet. I scooped him up with a hard swat while drivers shouted at me. He started crying and when we got back to the yard Cathy was crying not knowing where we'd gone, so I sat on the back step and joined them. When we had all had a good cry, we resumed our day!

There was a little country store on the far side of the orchard from us and more than once Mike managed to walk there, climb up on the bar stool and wait to be served at which point I would get an angry phone call to come get him. Because of his bright red hair everyone knew who he was and where he belonged. Fortunately, the store was on the same side of the highway as our house.

Moving to the new house was a bit more of the same as Mike really loved to explore but soon his red hair would give him away and someone would call saying, "There's a little redhead down the hill under the railroad trestle. Could that be your child?" Eventually John (Ed) got the yard fenced and built a playhouse/fort and a swing set he and I put together, finishing by flashlight! Then most of the neighborhood came to our house to play.

Across the street lived a family with one girl and three boys. As it turned out, Yoko, the mother had attended Visalia High with me. We were happy to renew our acquaintance. Since they were Japanese, her children went to a Saturday class to learn Japanese. Joan and Shin were exactly the same age and she begged to go to Japanese language school with him. Lots of tears! When Joan had her tonsils and adenoids out at three and a half he came over every day to sit with her and look at books. Lots of good memories at that house; a vegetable garden and always sweet peas and roses.

Meadow Way, Watsonville house under construction 1959.

Meadow Way house completed.

A CLEAN HOUSE

Growing up in one very old house
Never noticing the inside surroundings.
Only knowing they always had to be clean.

Then marrying and moving again and again;
Two of us, then 3, 4, and 5 from one place to another,
Until moving into our own home, carrying all in a car of green.

Along the way buying a lot on a hill
Sitting in wildflowers eating lunch as the children play
Watching the foundation of a house grow into my dream.

Through the winter while teaching school
Pregnant, with toddlers, trips to construction underway
Finally our own house finished March '59; I know, it still has to
be clean.

CHAPTER FIVE

THE SIXTIES

The Sixties started smoothly enough, settling into our own home and no babies in '60, '61 or '62. I distinctly remember sitting on the step in our garage holding our youngest, Joan, born in April '59 and watching Cathy, Mike and Terri play. I thought it much too cold a summer day to play outside, coming from the San Joaquin Valley, and thinking "This is where I belong! No more teaching for me." The four were a handful. Cathy stayed close to me and before Mike could walk always told others "This is my only faire brother." Once Mike could navigate on his own, he was hard to keep up with. We lost him once in Big Basin Park as he had run ahead and missed the turn off. Fortunately, he finally realized he'd gone too far and turned back. He reunited with us and the girls just before dark and just as I had engaged a ranger to help look for him. Terri was as independent as Mike but not nearly as mobile. Joan held on tight being very content as long as she was curled up under my chin; we six did lots of one day hiking and picnicking in the summers of '61 and '62, with weekly trips to the beach.

But I got restless and longed for the classroom. I signed to teach half-day summer school in '62 at Pajaro School district, and my sister, Betty, came to live with us for the six weeks. The folks had given us a rather high-strung dog the previous Christmas who loved to chase cars. That proved to be his demise that summer. I remember I earned enough to buy a Kitchen Aid mixing machine, which still works, and to pay Betty. My mom thought I badly shortchanged my sister! She didn't know how little teachers got paid! That fall I was again expecting, though I continued to substitute teach. We got a new car—a station wagon—more suited to six people. Terri and Joan stayed next door with Fern Peterson. Her youngest of three children was Stanley, the same age as Cathy, and she loved having the girls over even when they decorated her bathroom walls with drawings!

By June 1963 Carol was born and Cathy was old enough to be a great help with the others. After feeding Carol her early morning feeding around 5:30 or 6:00 I would go back to sleep and wake around 8:30 to see Cathy serving breakfast to Mike, Terri and Joan; carefully managing the half gallon milk

Summer 1961.

Easter 1963.

container filling each one's cereal bowl. The next fall Cathy and Mike were attending Moreland Notre Dame grammar school in Watsonville and Terri was going to Moss Landing kindergarten. I still remember Terri coming off the bus telling me President Kennedy had been shot! I admonished her not to joke about such things at which she got furious saying the teacher had announced that news; when we turned on the TV, I had to apologize.

Easter 1964.

Around Christmas John started looking for a better paying job which he found in Salinas with D'Arrigo Bros. From then on life became hard work! In February of 1964 we moved into a house on Riker Street, a house Ed had found and I had not seen; never again, I told

Last family photo before Bill's death, 1963.

my husband. It was here in the spring that we met Mrs. Thompson our next-door neighbor who became a beloved foster grandmother. Janet was born in March of 1965 and was not a well baby.

All our married life up to 1965, I had prepared the income taxes but this year John did them. Lo and behold we were chosen for an audit. We gathered all the papers and sent them in. All were accepted and approved. In going through them to put away, I found a pet veterinarian bill in with our doctor bills so felt we got away with something.

By Thanksgiving we were off to Fresno. Knowing I would have to change doctors, I had Janet checked as she still cried a lot and seemed miserable. The doctor said I was a crabby tired mother and Janet was fine. The drive over Pacheco Pass that rainy night was harrowing! John (Ed) in the pickup ahead with Mike and Terri and me following with Joan, Carol and Cathy holding Janet in the back seat. Janet cried most of the way and at the time the road had no shoulder as a pipeline was being laid. We drove to Visalia to my folks, as the family in Fresno had not vacated our house yet. Cathy must have been exhausted! Mom and Dad put us up for Thanksgiving and maybe the next week. Our things arrived that week and, I remember, the men had packed lunch boxes just as they had come home from school ten days before. What a mess! Janet cried most of Sunday night in our new home. Luckily a grammar school nurse friend, Shirley, lived in Fresno and put me in touch with the best doctor of my whole life experience. When I got her there and he drew blood, tested it and said, "You have a very sick baby here!" In my frustration I yelled at him. "I know that! That's why I'm here." He did not take offense just prescribed medicine, her iron count was half what it should be. Soon Jan was a happy baby opening the kitchen drawers and using them for stairs to climb on, so she could walk on the counter. None of the others had done that!

While living in Salinas, one set of friends we made that have lasted to this day, were Bob and Sue and their three daughters. We still kept up with Jolly and Dulce, Helen and Emil, Sandy and Al, Caroline and Jack, all from the babysitting co-op in Watsonville. Bob was a Chualar farmer who had his pilot's license. The spring after

Bob and Sue Johnson with me and John-Ed.

we moved to Fresno, Bob flew his family of five over to visit. All of us were thrilled, me especially! I dearly needed a friend. I got a babysitter for the nine of our kids and we went out to dinner. I remember being embarrassed to tell Sue I was expecting again. They did not abandon us and when we moved back to Salinas, we picked up right where we left off.

Soon John was transferred from Fresno to Brentwood, California and the children and I were alone remodeling a part of the house so Cathy and Mike could each have more privacy. We celebrated Christmas, 1966 with John's parents coming bearing many gifts. Lisa arrived January 11, three weeks early, and again I called on my sister Betty who was a student at Fresno State to come for the night we were both gone. John stayed home till I got out of the hospital, then was back to Brentwood. Lisa, more sickly than Janet, had to have lab work everyday for a week at which time it was determined she did not need a complete blood transfusion. My friend

Shirley and her two-year-old Tom, Carol, Janet, Lisa and I made the trek to the lab daily. Dr. Gerdes had already told me that because of my RH Neg. blood I should have no more children and thankfully we all agreed.

That year was long and tedious. In the summer John was offered his job at D'Arrigo Bros. back. He presented the prospect to the children and all of us were elated to go back to friends and familiar places. His parents helped us secure a lot to build on as we could not find a five-bedroom house to buy. Building started in September 1967 and in early December my parents came to stay with the children for two nights so I could go to Salinas to pick out wall papers, counter tops, carpet and paint colors for a five-bedroom, three-bath house in one long day. I did, and drove back to Fresno the next day. The following day while driving the children around Fresno, my neck was so stiff I could not turn it. So, while crossing Shaw Avenue, I had Cathy look to the right and Mike to the left so they could tell me when there was a lull in traffic and we could cross! My Guardian Angel was working overtime!

We were to move two more times, but finally settled at 689 Santa

689 Santa Monica Way house.

Monica Way in March of 1968 to stay. We left Fresno in late January and lived for six weeks on Harris Road with most of our things in storage. Anything lost or misplaced during those six-weeks—"must be in storage, Mom." All were delighted when moving day came, the kids could ride their bikes to Sacred Heart School. We were in our first two-story house and despite our best intentions the very first morning, fourteen-month-old, Lisa rolled all the way down the stairs, fortunately breaking nothing. Money was tight, I set about sewing drapes for the whole house finishing sometime in 1969.

Mike finished Sacred Heart sixth grade and started Palma in the fall of '68. Cathy graduated 8th grade in June '69 and started Salinas High though she would have preferred Notre Dame. We could not afford any more tuition and felt Mike needed more male company. Both could walk to their schools.

Sometime during this two-year period I saw the doctor who had called me a "crabby tired mother" when Janet was a few months old, at church. He waited till after Mass and just as I was going to my car, came up and apologized. He was now retired and seemed relieved to be able to set things right. What a surprise!

How I missed our first home at 15 Meadow Way, Watsonville, our group of friends and our neighbors. We had established ourselves in town as a reliable family, much like the reputation I had come from as a Hutcheson in Visalia.

The Catholic school was over enrolled with 70 children in each grade. Mike, who was not particularly interested in school, suffered greatly. When we got to Salinas, February '64, his second-grade teacher, Mrs. Guthrie, called to ask if she could keep Mike after school each day, as he did not know how to read at all. I had been too busy to notice!

Guardian Angel, 'Walking With'

Angel of God, my guardian dear
To whom God's love commits me here
Ever this day, be at my side
To light to guard, to rule and to guide.

Though I have neglected you rather much I fear
I know with each new soul, God creates an angel peer
To travel with, wherever they wander, even world-wide;
To bring them home at the end of their ride.

To have a reliable companion it seems
Is the longing in many a peoples' dreams
S/he is "walking with" us daily, though invisible
Till at last we realize we two are really indivisible.

How can I thank you for all of your care, wisdom and truth;
Except to offer love and understanding to the next set of youth.

MEMORIES OF UNCLE GEORGE

Holidays, Mom with Uncle George.

My Uncle George was the epitome of adventure! The story goes that he stowed away on a freighter out of a Texas port at sixteen and somehow landed in California. I don't know how he met my dad's sister, Aunt Peggy, but my first memory of him is when he was working in a bank and she was teaching school. She and her sister, Gertrude, had bought a lot in Visalia and built a duplex on it. Aunt Peggy wouldn't get married until she and Gertrude were all moved in.

As a child mostly I remember the Thanksgiving parties at our house on the ranch. After dinner Uncle George would come outside and turn the jump rope 'hot pepper' for ages, doling out nickels to those who jumped the longest. He was always laughing!

Then at nine I broke my right arm near the shoulder so was put in an upper body cast for about six weeks. In the valley, it was around 110 degrees all July and August so for most of the six weeks I stayed at Uncle George and Aunt Peggy's house because they had a "swamp cooler" to keep the house cool. They had lots of books and I read Black Beauty that summer. I was still enthralled with horses though falling off one was how I broke my arm. Uncle George was mostly a silent presence in the house. He would make his kids and me all laugh and act up, while Aunt Peggy was all business.

Uncle George showing off gold tooth.

The summer I turned fourteen and graduated eighth grade, Uncle George and Aunt Peggy were deeply involved in their country store (or he was) across from the local cannery where peaches and apricots were processed. That year they opened a diner adjacent to the store which Aunt

Peggy ran. The main meal was served at two a.m. when the night shift got their dinner break. By this time, my aunt and uncle had four children, three boys and a girl. I was hired as a live-in babysitter all summer — well for the seven or eight weeks of canning season. It was hot so we kept the shades drawn and played games in the darkened house till well past midday. On Sundays all went to church and if the boys acted up, as they usually did, Aunt Peggy would threaten them with a spanking. She demanded Uncle George deliver this punishment with a wide leather razor strop. He would argue with her. "They weren't so bad." I remember him being in utter anguish about it and begging her to let it go. I would have to go out on the back porch but could still hear the boys scream, an almost every Sunday occurrence. The next summer I got a job at the Assessor's Office at the court house where Mom had worked after high school.

When I graduated from high school, I began to work as a clerk at Uncle George's store on weekends through my two years of junior college. I loved working at the store with Uncle George; I mostly worked checking out customers while he stocked shelves, arranged produce and the meat counter. He swept the floors and sidewalk out front. Not a big man, 5'9 or 10" he was always gracious and jolly. His humor was genuine, never cruel or dirty. To tally people's bill, we had a hand crank adding machine. One was to clear the tape before starting each customer's bill by ringing up a 'no sale' which put a star at the top of the tape. This insured each customer only paid for their own items; not any previously rung up. One day I forgot to clear the tape and rang up groceries totaling over $100 as I recall. Seldom did we sell such a big amount to one person. When I tore off the tape, handed it to the couple and started to bag the groceries, she accused me of charging her for others' groceries as there was no star at the top of the tape. So, I had to start over and ring up each item again.

To my relief the tape totaled the exact same amount to the penny. Uncle George never said anything but I could feel his approval as he hovered in the background.

Every Sunday he went home for lunch and a nap from noon to three o'clock so I ran the store alone. One Friday after school Uncle George phoned me to ask if I'd taken a check last Sunday — $20 or $25 dollars as I remember. I said, "Yes." I could see in my mind's eye the two guys who only bought a pack of cigarettes. He told me the check bounced. I was mortified and offered to have him take the sum out of my wages, but he said "No, I just was not to accept any checks from now on." His way of teaching a lesson was gentler than his wife's, by far.

After I went away to San Jose State, I only remember him at family gatherings and holiday dinners — sometimes at our house and sometimes at theirs. He no longer would turn the jump rope but would pester my mom to sing with him or dance around the kitchen. He had a gold tooth right in the front and when he smiled it would just sparkle. He made sure the gatherings were fun (FUN) while Aunt Peggy was deeply involved in some serious discussion about politics on which no one could agree.

Uncle George died the year I was 36. We nine were living in a rental in the country while waiting for our new house to be completed in Salinas. On March 5, 1968, we bundled our seven children for the drive from Salinas to Visalia for the funeral. I needed to tell Uncle George goodbye. On March 13th we moved into our new home, Lisa, the baby, just fourteen months old. We had moved four times and had two children in the recent four years but mostly I remember '68 as the year Uncle George died! Somehow the FUN went out of life for quite awhile. It's been over 50 years since he died. His memory comes back to remind me, "Have FUN! Fun makes the journey and you much more enjoyable."

THE BLUE PRINT COTTON LINEN DRESS

Some people disturb—disrupt one's very plan for life! It isn't like they intend to, nor did you mean to let them, but they do.

On looking back, I can see what a huge thorn I was in my mother-in-law's side. I learned years after the first time I met her, that my now husband had gone home for the weekend in the fall of his junior year in college and told her he'd met the person he was going to marry. Many months afterward when I finally met her, I sensed I was not welcome. She didn't know me at all, but gave me the distinct impression she didn't want to know me. At that time, I didn't think marriage was for me or rather—I knew it was, but found the whole idea unattractive. I tried, over a two-year period, to disengage, but instead found I really was falling for this guy in spite of myself and in spite of the cold shoulder I experienced when visiting his home.

After almost three years we were married, much against her will. At the last minute, she agreed to attend our wedding but cried for hours (my mother said) after we left for our honeymoon. Her son had done the unthinkable; he had married a Catholic and even joined that faith.

As children began arriving things seemed to get better. She was extremely talented in all household arts: making yeast breads, knitting, sewing, crocheting as well as gardening. She still had two children at home and redoubled her efforts to have them turn out according to her prescribed plan. I felt though, that because my husband was her first and

Clockwise from left, Mildred, David, Mary, John, Joan , Cathy, Terri, and Mike. Christmas 1962.

favorite, she never fully recovered. We moved several times from San Jose to Watsonville to Salinas, to Fresno and back to Salinas. With each move came a new baby so these were hard times for me. I was so busy I just forgot to be bothered by Mildred's attitude. When we moved to Fresno with six children it was Thanksgiving and the baby at that time was very sick so all my energy was concentrated on getting a doctor and registering the older four at a school. Mildred and John Sr. came to visit in the spring, and stayed in a nearby motel for the weekend. They came for dinner on Friday though Ed didn't get home from work till after dinner was over. I was a nervous wreck trying to get everything done and running late. I still remember fixing Spanish rice and having no grated cheese for the topping, I just laid slices of American cheese on top of the rice. It definitely was not the same. I apologized feeling very inadequate. My father-in-law said "Never apologize for a meal. Be glad you have one." or words to that effect. I took these words as praise of a kind. The next day I had arranged for our new piano to arrive. I knew my husband's mother so loved to hear her son play. The delivery was so late his folks were ready to go back to the hotel but then it arrived. We all sat and enjoyed John's playing for quite a while. It was a happy ending to their visit and all the children were mesmerized.

I think it was during this visit that Mildred asked to take my measurements. I didn't think anything of it. She and John Sr. came back again just before Christmas that year ('66) and brought a Christmas stocking for each child with their name on it and a bathrobe for me as I was again expecting in January. She had also made poinsettias for a center piece for our Christmas table. They were assembled of red and green felt, gold beads, wire and florist tape. Beautiful! As I said she was very talented!!

Our seventh and final child arrived January 11, 1967, three weeks early and very sickly. Alas, John had been transferred to Brentwood so was only home in Fresno for the weekends. I really hadn't bought myself any clothes nor given any thought to that part of my life. The seven children and I were all about survival. In that early spring — about Easter time, I received a box in the mail from Mildred. It contained a made to order fitted cotton linen dress. It was a floral print on a sky-blue background — my favorite color — with a blue leather belt that she had also made, accompanied by a cardigan three quarter sleeve moss green hand knitted angora sweater. It had a label inside that said, "Made especially for you by Mildred Marcroft." The dress had a wide cowl neck and fit me to a "T." It didn't wrinkle and I wore it everywhere I went, shopping for the children's shoes, clothes, or groceries, to church or doctor visits. Though there were no words exchanged I felt I had definitely and finally been accepted! Being accepted had always come easy to me and because I had to work at it for twelve years, my acceptance was all the more precious.

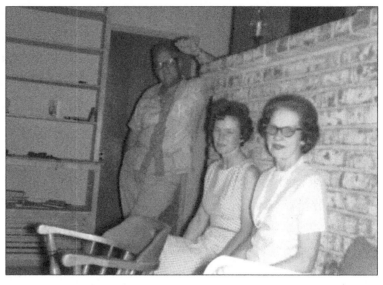

Grandpa John, me and Mildred, Fresno, 1966.

When John announced he had been asked to come back to Salinas all were overjoyed. For my in-laws, who had always lived in Redwood City, Salinas would be so much closer. By January of 1968 we had moved back even though our new house was not yet complete. We settled for a former foreman's house on Harris Road outside of Spreckels for six weeks. It meant another move but no one minded as we were back on the coast. In March of '68 we settled into our new two-story home where we lived for the next twenty-four plus years. My in-laws came to see us there later that month. In April, they asked us to come to Redwood City for a day, as Mildred was ill. When we left, she came to her door and said quite convincingly, "I'll be better the next time you come." Two weeks later we got the call, she had died. Both of us were shocked as were the children. To this day, I am grateful for her change of attitude and particularly for the blue print cotton linen dress! I can still picture it in my mind!

CHAPTER SIX

THE SEVENTIES

At a glance the seventies are just a blur, worse than the sixties if that's possible. This decade was also full of change—not academic or geographic as in my first two decades, not adjusting from mental to physical challenges as the second half of the fifties and almost all of the sixties, changing diapers and changing addresses. This kind of change was all consuming; changes in energy, attitudes, interests, relationships and responsibilities. There were changes in how to manage money, time and space. Starting in late '69 or early '70 I entered the literal "change of life" and became depleted, depressed and despondent telling God angrily each night, "Don't wake me tomorrow." This attitude went on for two years give or take a few months. I could not have been fun to be around. Little did I realize one does not give God orders; that's just not how it works.

Money was still short. Each week I made out the menu for the following week and from that, the grocery list. I balanced the checkbook to the penny, and the younger girls and I went grocery shopping on Fridays. Toward the end of the month I would hyper ventilate as I negotiated at the checkout counter hoping I would not have to put anything back to keep from overdrawing on the bank account. Occasionally there was enough to buy a pack of gum for the older ones to share. Anything that broke stayed broken.

Things were not easy for John either. D'Arrigo Bros. was one of the big growers whose laborers the United Farm Workers Union was trying to organize. Their tactics were ruthless and demoralizing. Since John was in charge of pest control for the crops, he became the main negotiator of the terms of the contract dealing with pesticides, causing him to be in meetings well into the night. At the same time, he was writing letters to the editor about his views of the Union and speaking on a radio show most Sundays against unionizing. Since I came from a farming background I too wrote letters, which did not get printed.

From the time we got to Salinas in '68, a friend from prior Salinas days, Gwen and I started a cadet Girl Scout troop for junior high girls, though it obviously was for us to meet other adults. I enrolled Terri and Joan in Junior Girl Scouts and Mike in Boy Scouts. Cathy stayed involved through her freshman year, which ended with a June trip on the cruise ship, the Matson Line's SS Lurline, on its final trip from San Francisco to Los Angeles. She did not have my adventurous spirit and did not particularly want to go but I insisted. Her father had been on this ship's initial trip as a six-month old from San Francisco to Honolulu in 1932 and I thought of it as a family honor. That one year there were six of us in scouting, as Carol had become a Brownie the fall before.

It was either that summer or the one before when Mike's troop did their fifty-mile hike in the Sierras. He had been very sick at the end of the school year with a bad case of canker sores in his throat. He could hardly swallow and I hesitated to let him go but the doctor said if he wants to go let him because he would hate me for keeping him home. Mike went and had a real adventure. One night, being too tired, he forgot to hang up his pack. The next morning, they found a bear had taken it out from under his head, ripped it open and eaten all the meals he was carrying. The troop had to come out a day early, as they had no food for the last day. Looking

Family photo, 1968.

'All for One and One for All'

First Class Scouters Cathy Marcroft, left, Virginia Croswhite, Kathy Gilmore and Janet Ryan clasp hands to symbolize "All for One and One for All." They recently earned Girl Scouting's highest award of First Class. Members of Spreckels Cadette troop 3104 and leader Mrs. Robert L. Todd will honor the girls, their first First Class Scouts, during the Court of Awards scheduled tomorrow evening at Spreckels School. The honored girls' parents also will participate in a special ceremony and refreshments will feature a cake made to duplicate the First Class patch. (Californian photo)

Salinas Californian, May 1970.

at the torn backpack almost sent me into shock!

At some point I became troop leader for Terri and Joan's troop, taking over twenty 5th and 6th grade girls overnight camping not one year but two. Once I remember putting the matches in my purse and using it for a pillow, thinking the girls could not start breakfast fires without my knowing it. I awoke to the smell of eggs cooking. Joan had graciously retrieved the matches from under my head and passed them around for all to light their burners. The next year, it rained and there were two troops of us at Camp Kawatre. One of the girls' fathers had given me a piece of plastic, which we'd strung over a rope between two trees. It was long enough to tuck under the head and foot of twenty-three sleeping bags, side by side. The other lady and I slept inside my station wagon with the tailgate open. We all felt pretty smug, as we were dry the next morning and watched the other soaking wet troop leave early. I quit being a leader after that but served on the local board accumulating ten years in scouting.

In July of 1971, I had my 40th birthday and reached the low point of my life. John knew I liked parties and so tried to cheer me up by throwing me a surprise party — and what a surprise it was! John had a huge guest list, too large for our modest size living room and he built a nice fire in the fireplace (it was July). People moved out to the front porch and all seemed to go pretty well till he ran next door and returned with the birthday cake.

Family photo, 1971.

It was decorated with "The Old Woman who lived in a shoe; She had so many children, she didn't know what to do." It would have been funny, if it weren't so true. People laughed, ate their cake and went home. The next morning, I loaded the five youngest in the car (Cathy and Mike had summer jobs in the field) and drove to Visalia. I don't know what my mother thought when we drove in, nor do I remember anything else about that incident.

John was under great pressure to stop writing letters to the paper denigrating the Union. Later that month, he was called into the office and basically quit and was asked to resign at the same time. When he returned for dinner, he suggested we have a drink. This was highly unusual, so I asked, "Are we celebrating or commiserating?" He said "Celebrating!" Here we are with seven children, sixteen and under, a fairly new mortgage and no job.

Within two and a half days, John got a call from a company he'd never heard of, asking him to take care of its' thousands of acres of row crops, pest wise. John and I decided to take what little savings we had and put a down payment on a pickup with a car radio. He would be in business for himself and charge by the acre of crop he walked. I would type and send out bills, do the banking and keep the books. But still we were scared! I decided to substitute teach during the '71-'72 school year (just in case this didn't work out) and maybe it would lift my mood. We set up John's office beside the kitchen table and began. Starr, next door agreed to keep Lisa on the days I substitute taught. I would get the call by 6:30 a.m., call Starr and start breakfast while making lunches for six children and myself, (Starr fed Lisa). I had to drop Cathy at Salinas High, Mike at Palma, the other four at Sacred Heart and get to my appointed school by 8:30. Once teachers found I would take sixth grade, I got a call more days than not.

This whole operation began October 1, 1971 and I lasted till mid-April, 1972. During these few months I was also head negotiator with the Salinas School District for a pay raise for substitutes, which meant night meetings once or twice a month. We got the raise and other farmers started calling John to walk their fields. By March 1st, he'd made as much as his whole twelve months the year before! I quit substituting, and started getting things fixed, starting with the house.

The oldest four children were as tall or taller than I was, so the dining room and kitchen as well as the living room had all become too small. Things were going at such a fast pace, we all operated on trust - I trust you will do as we agreed and be where we agreed at the pre-appointed time. I remember wondering on some mornings when things were very hectic, "Who will be the adult today?" And it wasn't always John or me. The children still talk about the list of chores in the kitchen. Every Saturday everyone had a job. You could choose your job and sign up but the next week you got a different one, as some seemed easier than others. I learned this from Girl Scouts; some jobs were inside, others outside. Everyone worked together Saturday mornings till all was done; lawns mowed and house cleaned.

By May first we agreed we had to rearrange and add on to the house and it seemed the money (carefully managed) was no issue. We contacted the people who had built the house, Hampshire Construction Co. and went to work. We switched Mike's bedroom to the dining room in the front of the house and knocked out a supporting wall between his room and the living room, making one large living-dining room. Then on the kitchen side of the house, we added a twenty by twenty-foot family room open to the kitchen. John was mostly gone, so the foreman and I went shopping for the wall paneling and the light fixtures and flooring. That foreman and I could have built lots of houses as we got along so well. Since we had no furniture except John's desk and my typewriter it was his office for a while. One year it was packed with cases of Girl Scout cookies when I was Girl Scout cookie chair for Salinas and South County. Since the kitchen was torn up for a week some of the girls took the Greyhound bus to Mom and Dad's and the rest of us camped out meal-wise.

Having this adjustment in space helped immensely but Cathy and Mike reaching sixteen meant all new challenges, like finding time for driving lessons (John was usually gone to the fields) and it also meant the beginning of dating! Cathy and Mike soon were "going steady." Looking back, I see I was more into efficiency than affection and tension was evident between John and I. I wonder if that tension at home encouraged outside relationships somehow?

Driving lessons had their challenges! One drizzly Saturday afternoon I let Joan drive home on River Road, though she did not yet have her driver's permit. When I asked her to slow down and seeing a car coming from the other direction, she over corrected taking out a fence post and the attached barbed wire. We flew out into a young bean field landing right side up miraculously just between the rows of plants! One had only to drive straight ahead to exit the field, no harm done. John came and got us and the farmer was happy his beans survived but he wanted his fence fixed. The following Saturday Joan enlisted her brother and her dad's posthole digger and returned to the field. They reset the post and fixed the fence. One would have thought the farmer had never known a teenager to repair what they had broken; he bragged about the good work Joan and Mike had done and for ages, much to our chagrin, the news traveled far and wide among South County residents.

Next, I had major surgery and Cathy and Mike were called on to do a lot. In the fall of '72 Lisa started afternoon kindergarten. For a week or so my neighbor came over to fix our lunch and get Lisa ready for school. I can't remember how the others got to school, I think they must have walked or ridden bikes.

The next spring Cathy graduated from Salinas High School. She got a summer job at Dick Bruhn's and enrolled in Hartnell Junior College that fall. The children all had summer jobs as soon as they were old enough and the job of setting up bank accounts, saving and checking, and teaching each how to balance checking accounts fell to me. After one semester at Hartnell, Cathy got on full time at her job and John and her boyfriend had a disagreement. Then in the spring of '74 I came home one day to find Cathy's room empty — furniture, clothes and all! I did not know where she had moved and was frantic. It seemed she had an apartment across town but would not contact us on the advice of her boyfriend. He said we had other children and did not need her. I was in such pain, emotionally, mentally and physically I could not stand up straight or sleep. On the third night (per my habit when frustrated) I silently yelled at God saying, "If you want this family to stay together and with you, you do it! I quit!" I distinctly heard "I was wondering when you would ask for help." And I felt held in someone's arms as I fell asleep. Then I knew all these relationships would sort themselves out and concurrently experienced the greatest change of my life. I no longer made my plans and asked God to bless them; I asked God's plans for me and set about praying I could fulfill them.

By this time John had rented an office downtown and hired a secretary, much to my relief.

Inspired by Love after Love by Derek Walcott

It was one of my down times –I don't remember the year—when six of my seven children were still living at home. The oldest had left in the only way she saw possible; with a complete break in the relationship, which I'm sure from her viewpoint didn't really exist anyway.

I had started seeing a counselor during the day when all were in school. We lived in Salinas and she was on David Avenue in Pacific Grove. I can no longer remember her name, but she had been a teacher, retired and after more schooling had become a Marriage and Family Counselor. She was about twenty years my senior. During this time my husband was on the road with his job, four to five nights a week. Managing the house, the money and the activities of six others ranging from seven and a half to seventeen with no adults to discuss things with was beginning to get on my nerves plus I was very worried about the whereabouts and well being of my eighteen year old who had left so abruptly.

My biggest complaint to the counselor, as I remember, I expressed as being "very lonesome." One day after an hour of pure complaining and relating all the demands on my time and energy, to which she listened, really listened; I prepared to leave not feeling one bit better. I told her again I was just lonesome. I thought I was lonesome for my family, for friends from varying stages of my life, for the neighborhoods where we had lived and frankly for the solitude of the farm where I was raised. As I walked to the door, the counselor said, "I really don't see how you can be lonesome with all those children's love and hugs." I knew she was right, BUT ... and suddenly a light dawned! I was lonesome for myself, the Self who was currently nowhere in sight. Other than going to the counselor for one hour a week I had taken no time for myself in years—that Self who was fun loving and delighted in playing sports - any sport, or dancing - any kind. I resolved to treat myself better, soon telling the counselor that I wouldn't need her any more. Thank you!

Within two years our eldest had returned to the nest-a major blessing, and though my responsibilities and circumstances had not changed, I found a liturgical dance group and began tennis lessons-which immediately became my passion. In liturgical dance I learned ballet moves to hymns; a very healing way of praying with one's whole body. This movement enabled my mind to move out of its stuck position. The tennis and dancing also complemented each other. This was pointed out to me at one of the dance performances when at the end a gentleman asked if I also played tennis as he could see similarities in the moves. The third benefit was the great improvement in my state of mind—really an opening to God's grace—all thanks to the intriguing and enlightening insight I'd gained at counseling.

Love After Love by Derek Walcott

The time will come
when, with elation,
you will greet yourself arriving
at your own door, in your own mirror
and each will smile at the other's welcome,

and say, sit here. Eat.
You will love again the stranger who was your self.
Give wine. Give bread. Give back your heart
to itself, to the stranger who has loved you

all your life, whom you ignored
for another, who knows you by heart.
Take down the love letters from the bookshelf,

The photographs, the desperate notes,
peel your own image from the mirror.
Sit. Feast on your life.

WATER / MERCY

There is a necessary fluid that quenches: sometimes sparingly, after a slight shower, or on more fruitful days, after a deluge, and its clear sparkling liquid makes its way down hill forming a small but determined stream going forth to join others rushing to revive those of us grown dry and parched since last this melted flow passed our way. This is our most precious commodity, water. It, like mercy, is at times in short supply. Who owns what comes from below the earth, whose sandy soil lets it leech away quickly never really to be held or tasted? As with water, some are in dire need of mercy, some seemingly never desire it at all. Some are givers, some takers—will the takers eventually cause the stream to run dry, cause all to become hard hearted? Mercy, like water is absolutely necessary though not for the body as much as for the spirit. Without it we become dehydrated and brittle.

Within each of us is the hidden spring that can bubble up and fill the well. But it must be nurtured by the mercy of others, the compassion that encourages the drops to form and increase in number becoming a spring. It flows out of us as looks, then words, and then touches that inspire the spring to swell until it bursts out into the open enriching all in sight. A baby's first smile tells us the spring is there with the potential to grow. There are thousands, maybe millions, whose spring only nourishes themselves while riding the waves of struggle and strife we each encounter. Yet there are others of generous nature whose tiny spring has grown to a mighty river emptying into a huge lake. They call all in sight to come bath in me saying, "Make yourselves clean for the journey's end where all shall glisten as tears of gladness for having participated in this human community." We see each one of us so different from the other as to find incredulous the width and breadth, height and depth of all these acts of kindness, be they minute or magnanimous.

What is the medical recommendation for a healthy adult quantity of water per day—six eight oz. glasses? I don't recall any such daily doses recommended for mercy, but six sounds right— two approving glances, two sets of kind words and maybe two hugs. The only trouble is these are not readily available from the tap and they must first be given away before they can be received.

Remember though, mercy like water, is not just for others. It is OK even suggested, that each of us imbibe daily along life's path. Be good to yourself. These two quantities are much needed to sustain all life and enrich this human community. They are without doubt, the source of life, both physical and spiritual.

Parties and Other Diversionary Tactics

Regardless of all the serious drama, I'd somehow always known a good party could solve a lot of problems! My folks had always worked hard but also played hard! While in Watsonville, the babysitting group and preschool parents enjoyed several a year, plus square-dancing lessons together one summer. While at Riker Street in Salinas I only remember one birthday party for Mike and a Chinese New Year dinner party one year when Vince, my brother and his wife visited.

John and I and the children managed to attend the weddings of my three sisters and three brothers wherever we lived. We went to Redwood City for his sister's wedding. While in Fresno, I remember giving Cathy a slumber party in the sixth grade. That worked out so well, I continued the practice with each of the other girls. Having the new family room in summer of 1972 certainly helped. There we also had a Toastmasters party (John had joined a group the year before), eighth grade graduation parties, Mike's rehearsal dinner and our first grandchild's baptismal breakfast!

Early in the '70s John's dad had remarried a delightful woman named Bernice. We attended this wedding also which was a good time amidst some sad times; the death of my brother Bill and the loss of my sister Fran's ex-husband, Joe—two thirty-somethings' needless deaths causing funerals within six weeks of each other adding to our trying year of '71.

Bernice holding down the fort with Lisa (left) and Terri.

In the spring of '75 with Mike at Hartnell, two girls at Notre Dame High and the three youngest at Sacred Heart School, our beloved friends, Bob and Sue asked us to go to Puerto Vallarta for a week. The Lord knows we needed a vacation. Besides school, Carol was taking piano lessons, Janet dance lessons plus Joan's sports calendar at high school; escaping seemed impossible! Then Bernice came to mind. She and John's dad had only been married three and a half years when he had died in January '74. We had kept up with Bernice and included her in family events. I asked her if she would come stay a week at our house while John and I went to Mexico. She agreed immediately. I had only to get her a hair appointment at my hairdresser. No problem!

Bob and Sue Johnson, me and John in Puerto Vallarta, 1975.

We stayed on the beach in a thatched roof duplex with Bob and Sue, eating only breakfast of coffee and Mexican pastries, sometimes a fresh pineapple on the front deck. We swam most afternoons after a day of exploring and always had dinner out—what a treat for me! I admired people we saw parasailing and expressed a desire to do that. Since it was Sunday, Sue shooed us off to church saying they would secure a boat to take me up but she didn't want to tell the children we'd missed mass if anything happened to me. All this from a lady who had told me "religion was a crutch!" We met them at the beach and I had the ride of my life,

Parasailing.

sailing six hundred feet above the ocean and beach. It was the most peaceful respite I had in twenty-one years. I hated to come down but did, gently landing on my feet on the beach. We watched, as the next customer was strapped in wearing an expensive watch and with a camera around his neck. The boat took off lifting him only a few feet off the water when the engine failed and the man slowly sank into the Bay of Banderas. He had to walk ashore soaked to his ears. Mass must have helped!

Other fun times were the two or three yearly potlucks we six couples in the corner of Santa Fe and Santa Monica Way had; two couples in their sixties, two of us in our mid-forties and two just under thirty. We had nothing in common except we were neighbors who enjoyed each other's company and food. Russells, who lived across the street were retired and so a favorite target of Janet's. She would somehow get Lisa across to their driveway when I was busy and ask if Mr. Russell could play? She had discovered he was usually home and kept candy bars in his garage workbench drawer. After their "party" Etta would call to say the girls were over there, if I had not already missed them.

One night while saying goodbye at the front door, neighbor Merle, carrying his wife's empty dish, suddenly thrust the dish into John's hands, grabbed me and kissed my cheek, took his dish back and walked down the steps. John wasn't happy but it had happened so fast he'd not had time to react. Merle was one of the older men so I just laughed while his wife reprimanded him on their walk home. We twelve had a lot of laughs!

We celebrated our 25th wedding anniversary on Santa Monica Way, and the children gave us a surprise 35th anniversary party there as well. It really was a successful surprise as well as a much needed good time.

The only way I can possibly get a handle on this party topic is to organize it by decades. The ones with the most parties were definitely the happiest! Actually, that sounds like "parties as a way of life," but that's not true; one could only play hard provided one had worked hard.

In my second decade, the one and only party was when I turned thirteen and it was the absolute best. I was attending a small private school and there were only thirteen in my class, four girls and nine boys. We invited the whole class to dinner and the show. In the summer our family ate on the screened in porch, as it was so hot in the valley. I think only ten came and my mother and two others put on a full three-course meal ending with birthday cake and homemade ice cream. Then two cars of us were driven the five miles into town, at the then speed limit of 35 mph, to the show. I don't remember what was showing, only that the theatre was air-conditioned and there were at least two boys to each girl. I surely felt like "Queen for the Day."

By the next decade I had married and discovered that my husband, who was born on February 29th, had never had a birthday party. Since he would be six that year it seemed the perfect time to rectify this omission. We invited our current friends, mostly his fraternity pals from San Jose State and reminded them the party was for a sixth birthday. We played "Pin the Tail on the Donkey" and other childish games but the most memorable part was the gifts. One brought a goldfish bowl complete with two goldfish but the most noteworthy was a straight jacket from the then Agnews, a mental hospital in San Jose. What sort of child had he been?

Family photo, 1977.

The next decade was filled mostly giving parties for the children. We had by this time settled in Salinas and after four years added a family room, 20′ by 20′, to our downstairs. So, each child had an eighth-grade graduation party. One of the most memorable was Joan's. One of the boys brought a six-pack of beer, which my husband confiscated at the front door. As the children were leaving John tried to give the six-pack back but the young man said, "No way, I can't take that home!" We had a good laugh and a six-pack of beer. Then there were the high school parties; I learned what marijuana smelled like and why I should never leave home on weekends.

During this time John belonged to the Sunrise Toastmasters Club, as did our neighbor, Jack. Once a year the club invited their wives and had a dinner party. This year, Jack's wife, Starr, and I decided we would give the party. We picked a Japanese theme, ordered Japanese food and since our big 20′ by 20′ room had no furniture, we scrounged pillows and set them out in clusters of four so all could sit on the floor and eat. Following the Japanese tradition, we had all remove their shoes when they entered the house. Just inside the door John had placed two huge cardboard barrels and guests were instructed to put one shoe in each barrel. I had fed the children early and moved the TV upstairs and they reported all went well until we started our games after dinner.

This house had two large rooms, on either side of the stairs, that led up from the front door — the new family room and a living-dining room. One could walk from one to the other through the kitchen or down the hall under the stairs. We divided the guests into two teams and place one team and one barrel in each of the large rooms. They had to dump out the barrels and find their one shoe, rush to the other room and find their other shoe and get back to the room they had started in. The first team to

45th Wedding anniversary, 1999.

The little people at anniversary party, 1999.

complete the process won. The children said we were so loud they talked about calling the police! Thank goodness calmer heads prevailed!

The years of '71–'80 were pretty much without parties. John had his own business where he traveled half of almost every week and we had seven children to educate. In the decade of '81 –'90, I finished my Masters, all had graduated from college and two of our children had achieved Masters degrees. We had three weddings and those parties the children really managed; we just paid for them. We set a sum and each one decided how many guests, how much food and what kind of music they could buy with it. And of course, they could add to it.

In the '90s we had three more weddings and the grandchildren began coming, which was all very exciting and lessened my need for parties. We also began to travel quite a bit. On our forty-fifth anniversary we decided to give ourselves a party. We had a late afternoon mass followed by dinner at Corral de Tierra. This was special to me as my parents and John's never made it to their 45th anniversary. The priest, Fr. Mike Miller, surprised us by asking us to give the reflection during the mass. I went first and as I began to speak, our two-year-old granddaughter Rebecca came up and stood at the lectern with me. When I finished, she and I returned to our seats as though it was planned.

At Corral I had arranged a sit-down dinner with tables of eight where I had placed cards seating people at certain tables. We had people from throughout our life who may not have known each other so I tried to scatter our children and their spouses around the room to make all comfortable with their dinner companions. The weirdest things happened! At one table were a daughter and her husband, her cousin and his wife and two couples in their late 70's. They discovered they had all graduated from Santa Clara University in different years. At another table I had unwittingly seated people who at college had been student and professor. At another there were two farmers who had not seen each other in forty years. And, so it went. The children wrote a song about us to accompany a familiar tune and the band played it. The same band, by the way, that played for most of the weddings. The priest who had baptized most of the children while we lived in Watsonville drove up from Barstow to attend. There was a lot of Spirit (with a capital S) to go with the liquid spirits at that party! This party was a great healer and went a long way to bringing John and me closer.

For our 50th anniversary, we all stayed at a hotel in Aptos, California for two nights. We hired a photographer to take pictures and I asked the grandchildren to provide entertainment, which to everyone's delight, they did. Uncle Jim videotaped it, a treasure to be sure!

Listening

How often have you been listened into existence?
I dare say, "Not often enough",
especially when the moment before did not seem special
or serious or about to become indelible.
But the fact that you remember it, says someone cared
enough to listen and to respect your words as gospel.
Few have the knack for hearing what's behind the words—
to recognize
their sacredness, and by knowing their sacredness, know
ME, the speaker.
It is human to crave an audience but even more true that
we must be the audience in order to have one.

SWITCHBOARD OPERATOR

"Did you tell Dad?"

"Don't tell Dad!"

"Tell her to clean her room"

Suddenly I had a visual, plain as day. A lady sits in front of a board full of jacks with a light above each one. She wears headphones and a mouthpiece. She connects phone calls by inserting a pair of plugs into the appropriate jacks. Each pair of plugs is a part of a cord circuit with a switch that lets the operator participate in the call. The light above the jack lights up when a receiver is lifted. By listening to the caller, she can connect her/him with the person they wish to talk to.

This image came to me when our older children became teenagers and Ed was on the road a lot. It has stayed with me. I had not thought of myself that way before. He did not talk face to face to the children very often using me as intermediary. Since he was gone so much when he did call in, he usually talked to me. Realizing the unhealthiness of this practice, I have tried to discard it.

As I write this, and because of this recurring image, I find some history falling into place. Somehow authority, parental or otherwise, had never threatened me as it does some people, probably because my parents had never abused it with me. At boarding school, I was usually elected to go ask the teacher the question we all wanted an answer to, or the principal for permission for special favors for the boarders—"You ask, she likes you!" And again, way back in time, "Did you tell Mom? "Don't tell Dad!" "Can you talk to her/him for me?" As we left my house to begin our honeymoon, the parting words of one sister seemed harsh and incomprehensible. "Ed, you are breaking up our family!" After many years when celebrating my husband's 80th birthday another sister repeated those words verbatim and said in her toast to him, "You didn't break up our family, Ed, you doubled it!" Now I understand that as the oldest of eight, my sisters felt they were being abandoned by their intermediary, their switchboard operator was leaving!

Life's Lessons

One of life's most important lessons—at least one that has been most helpful—has been "How to treat people." In my life there are others and me. Somehow, I got the understanding early on, that both were equally important. Age, size, color and economic background were factors to be recognized but they had no bearing on day to day interaction with the people in my life. These factors did influence how one related to others; you didn't take candy from babies for instance or pick an argument with the class bully who was head and shoulders taller than you. One had tools to use in discerning how to treat people. One was the Golden Rule and the other was the premise "that ALL are created equal," meaning no one was greater or lesser in the eyes of God. Because of that belief, one knew and felt that each person has value including the self.

Developing this SELF required that other tools be accumulated and this involved listening obediently. Dad always said one could learn a lot from just listening, so I could be present at any and all of his meetings if I remained silent. His greatest regret was his limited education—eighth grade only, due to his father's early death—so he admonished each of us to pursue our studies diligently, with the end goal being the ability to discuss with others and to put into words one's own ideas and viewpoint. He felt others would be more respectful if one could converse in an educated manner while always looking them in the eyes. Anyone who looked away while he was talking to them was guilty of shiftiness and not to be trusted. I was an avid learner of Dad's ways. I continued to shadow Dad, as being out in the field with the men was so much more attractive to me than staying in the house learning the art of housekeeping. I sought class offices and opportunities to do public speaking in school. Inevitably things went wrong at times. Like when I was in 7th grade and taking ballroom dancing lessons one night a week in town. After Dad picked me up one night, we ran out of gas about half way home. We got out and walked, him telling me jokes and laughing along the two-mile hike in the dark. He was good at modeling the lessons he wished to teach; in this case how to deal with adversity. Of course, he was the one to walk back with gas, not so fun. Six or seven years later this experience came in handy as my boyfriend and I also ran out of gas a couple of miles from the house. I thoroughly enjoyed singing and dancing down the country road in my high heels in the dead of night. He was embarrassed by my "loudness" and did not see the fun and adventure in it at all.

My being a girl with all this training on how to meet the world did eventually cause trouble for both Dad and me. His cronies down at the country store warned him it was futile to educate girls. "They just get married and leave you, sooner or later." He spent many an hour over many a beer trying to prove his theory that girls as well as boys needed to be educated. Of course, the cronies were right, at least about girls leaving, but Dad was a good sport and walked me down the aisle with good humor while we both acknowledged that education lasts forever.

Being a married woman with all this training was just plain frustrating! Waiters in the '50s would always ask the gentleman how we liked our meal. I may as well have been a fly on the wall. Out of respect for current custom I would wait until the waiter left and then tell my husband what I thought of the meal. John listened patiently and did what was necessary to correct things. As children came and I no longer had the energy or time to teach, my frustration grew and became almost intolerable. As things progressed, I channeled my talents into arranging our social calendar, but being mostly at home and moving frequently that was not much of an outlet. My talents of being able to speak up and discern who was trust worthy were used to deal with moving companies, building contractors and repairmen. These activities coupled with managing the checkbook and expenditures while training seven children in the proper ways of being in the world were, though edifying, not along the lines of changing the world as I had hoped. I honestly thought my training would allow me to be taken seriously by men and women alike. Illusions of grandeur, YOU BET!

When my dad turned 62, he was operated on for esophageal cancer and lost his ability to speak. The cancer was from smoking. Mom phoned the day before the surgery and asked if I wanted to speak to Dad as I would never again be able to hear his voice but I couldn't take the time that day. I do not regret it as I can always hear his advice. In the next ten years after the surgery and before his death, he tried valiantly to continue to make himself understood but I sense he was as frustrated as I had become though I still had my voice. I wrote letters to editors and stayed involved in my children's activities, but mostly life had become about "keeping on keeping on" and having a good laugh and/or cry when things got too frustrating. I have learned to be a speaker at women's events which is very gratifying, but my ambitions to persuade men to see women as capable and as worth listening to as any man went down the tubes with the failure of the Equal Rights Amendment which, though passed by the House of Representatives in '71 and the Senate in '72, failed to obtain ratification by three-fourths of the states. From then on I concentrated on passing on my belief system to my son and six daughters. People do comment on my son's respect for women and on our daughters' responsible, respectful ways of being in the work world as well as in their homes. Dad would have been proud!

Keeping on!

The Coleman Pop-Up Tent Trailer

As soon as we knew John's business was a go, we bought a used Coleman Pop-Up Tent Trailer and made several trips with it. The trips sort of blend together now, one was to Lake Almanor where we could look up and see Mt. Lassen. Those of us who liked to climb decided it would be cool to climb the mountain and take pictures of the lake, as we had stood at the lake and taken pictures of the mountain. So, the next day we started out, going about a fourth of the way, and while stopping for a rest, Lisa the youngest asked where we were climbing to. When told "to the top of that mountain," she asked if we would be returning on this same trail? "Yes, of course." "Then," she announced, "I'll wait here." Since she was about five, we couldn't leave her on the trail but she was adamant about not climbing any further. I really wanted to say I had made it to the top so didn't want to stay with her. Finally, Terri thirteen or so, saved the day saying she would sit and play with her. They had to promise to stay in this one spot. All worked out but I was a nervous wreck leaving two children alone on the trail.

We went on to Diamond Lake, which was filled with frogs. They must have just matured from pollywogs because they were everywhere including in a lot of people's suits, making for lots of squeals and laughter.

Another trip we took was to the American River where we placed the tent trailer in a low spot. At the end of the week our station wagon would not pull it up to the road. We would still be there if not for a kind truck driver who hauled it up to a level spot where we could again connect and head home.

One of the best trips was to Lake Tahoe. On a given night we all cleaned up and went into Reno for a dinner show. As we walked in, the maitre d' approached and John asked for a table for nine up close to the front. He shook his head, saying those tables were all reserved, probably thinking the kids would not behave. Anyway, in the split second we stood there wondering what to do, Joan said, "Dad, slip him a fin!" For some reason, my husband dumbfounded at her choice of words and not used to following orders, did as she suggested. The maitre d' turned and lead us to the row just in front of the stage! We still don't know where an eleven-year-old got her language. The show's stars' names, with the exception of Flip Wilson, are lost to me now, but he was a G-rated comedian and all had a great dinner and a good time, thanks to a "fin" and an eleven-year old who spoke up.

One of the last trips I remember was to New Brighton Beach Camp Grounds. Only this time the four oldest all had summer jobs. John pulled the camper to the park and situated it next to my friend, Collene's. She had her three children, in the same grades as our three youngest, Carol, Janet and Lisa. She also had a dog with her. Our husbands left us there on a Sunday for a week. All went well till the middle of Saturday night when I was awakened by people crashing around through the brush, wild flashlight beams and Collene's dog barking. It seemed forever till all was quiet again. The dog quieted down when the movement outside stopped, but I didn't get much sleep that night. No cell phones. Collene and I could not contact each other or call a ranger, though I knew she was trying to keep the dog still. The Rangers were there as soon as we stirred the next morning and told us the offending people had been ushered out of the park. We thanked them for patrolling the campsites the night before. We were both glad to see our husbands pull up to take us home to Salinas.

LATE SEVENTIES

The summer of '75, I asked Carol and Janet if they wanted to play summer softball. When they said "yes" I signed them up to play Little League baseball. Yes, they were playing on the boys' team but they were just as good or better than some ten to twelve-year old boys. I never even questioned whether girls could join but they found they were the only girls on the team. First though they both needed new mitts. I gave them my credit card and off they went on their bikes to Stan Lisk's Sporting Goods Store. I phoned him and said the girls were coming and I would appreciate it if he would help them pick out softball mitts that fit them, as I was too busy to come myself. The girls came home with a shiny new mitt each saying, "If we could pick out our own grandpa, we would pick Mr. Lisk. Grandpa Marcroft had just passed away and my Dad was not well. I got one call from a coach worrying about the girls getting hurt but told him I felt they were no more likely to get hurt than one of the boys. As the season went on another call came when Jan had missed a game or two and the coach said, "We really need Jan! Please see that she is at the next game."

Mike, being at Hartnell that first year of college, took to umpiring, as he felt protective of the girls. He learned it wasn't the game the girls needed to be protected from it was the parents. He sent one father to his car for his remarks and I think he was a bit shook up at having to keep order during the game. The next summer there were three girls on Janet's

175

team and their team surprised the league coming in first. It wasn't long before the Bobby Sox league got started, mostly in North Salinas and the girls switched. There were a lot of cold evenings sitting in sleeping bags.

From then on life seemed all about college and college applications. Mike had decided Hartnell was not for him so set about getting into Fresno State. Then Terri decided on Santa Clara, a private school, Cathy returned home and applied to Long Beach State and when Joan applied to Fresno State and was accepted we, for one school year, had four in college. They had to get the grades and fill out the application; I just managed the money and transportation.

In the fall of '76 we had gone to the mountains to celebrate Thanksgiving and play in the snow but there was no snow. On our return Sunday night we discovered my dad had died. We rounded up all the children again and headed to Visalia for his funeral. Mom's Alzheimer's was progressing but so far, she could still stay at home and the six of us Hutchesons took every sixth weekend staying with her while Vince hired week day/night help to watch her. For Dad's funeral, Mom surprised my sister-in-law by pulling out a new black dress from her closet. No one could remember her buying it. At the funeral Dad was laid out in an open casket (probably not the best idea) because just before the service began Mom got up, went to the casket and gave Dad a kiss. She returned to her seat saying rather loudly, "My that was a cold kiss!" That was true so some of us giggled but others were offended by her remark. After another year or so, we agreed it was just too hard to care for Mom at home. We all investigated options in our own areas and decided to bring Mom to Katherine Convalescent Hospital in Salinas.

Vince and Betty moved into the folks' house on the ranch after we cleaned it out. On Easter Saturday all six of us Hutchesons met at the ranch and decided what we wanted, putting our color sticker on the piece. If two or three wanted the same piece we flipped a coin. Dorothy who lived back East had already asked Vince to pack up what she wanted so those things were already gone and our brother Bill had died, thus only six of us. The next morning, we returned with u-hauls (if needed) and after breakfast for all and an Easter egg hunt for the children we all left for home.

I visited Mom almost daily usually helping her through lunch at 11:30 as I started teaching afternoon preschool that next fall for three years. We sometimes brought Mom to the house for Sunday dinner and the girls and I usually arranged a birthday social for her at the hospital. Mom still loved to sing and knew the words to more songs than anyone so someone would play the piano and we, and the nurses present, sang the afternoon away. I learned those years that the words to songs are the first pieces our kids memorize and the last things that leave our memory.

Since 1974 when I resolved to do something for myself, I continued my tennis lessons and dance lessons. Since Ed started his own business, he had joined The Grower-Shipper Association, which always had a week long gathering in June with a golf tournament for the men, a tennis tournament for the women, a fashion show luncheon for the women and a formal dinner dance for the couples. I loved all the social events. We usually went to the dinner-dance with Bob and Sue. In 1977 I entered the tennis doubles tournament with Roberta and we won second place; had a formal picture taken and got mentioned in the local paper. I was on cloud nine!

In January 1979 Joan transferred from Fresno back to Hartnell. Terri had gone to Vienna, Austria the prior August and all were missing her; we decided to make the trip to visit. John could make a business trip out of his expenses, and as I was teaching preschool, which had a week-long spring break, we made plans for the two of us to go to Europe. We left

Joan in charge, with Carol in high school, Janet in eighth grade, and Lisa in sixth. Before we left I had a list of things to do, I had the living room, dining room and stairwell repapered and re-carpeted, finally I baked a rhubarb pie and froze it. Arriving in Vienna with my pie in hand, still frozen, the airport authorities wanted to know what was in the package. Looking in my German-English dictionary I could find no word for pie so mimed eating the package. He finally let us out of the airport to where Terri was waiting.

The trip was fun. Since we wanted to travel to Basel, Switzerland we rented a car and since John did not want to drive in Europe, I had obtained an international driver's license. After a couple of days in Vienna we were off to the Ciba-Geigy office in Basel. It was raining hard and we were in rural Germany when an officer stepped out into the road and signaled for us to stop. He fined me for speeding and when John instructed Terri to tell the officer in German, "That's a lot of money."

He said, "I'm only charging for speeding not for passing over a double yellow line." Too muddy to see any line! He pocketed the money and we were off again.

The gentleman at Ciba-Geigy was fascinating. He asked us if we wanted to converse in English, French or German. We said we were most comfortable in English, then we talked about pesticides for cotton whether grown in California, Egypt or Israel—a far cry from talking to preschoolers—and I knew about boll weevils in cotton in California. We saw a little of the town and were then off back to Vienna by a different route. Leaving Terri at her room we left for London on our way home where we were again treated royally, by Lloyds of London with whom John had also done business. I was the only woman at the business luncheon (all servants, silver and white linen) so was presented with a corsage when we were leaving. No other women on the streets of the business district either; things have changed in these forty-some years. We flew into SFO but had to take a bus to Gilroy where Joan and the girls met us. Hard on Janet as she had a big test the next day so didn't get much studying done.

Come June 26, 1979 we had lots to celebrate! It was our 25th anniversary, Mike had graduated from Fresno and had his first job, Cathy was home for the summer from Long Beach State, Terri was home from spending her junior year in Vienna, Janet had graduated eighth grade and with Carol a sophomore at Notre Dame High, Joan home and Lisa going into seventh grade, we decided to have a home mass with Fr. Ken Laverone to celebrate. Home masses were all the rage

25th Wedding anniversary, 1979.

then. Joan and Lisa picked out the readings and hymns. Carol's friend, Cindy, played the piano. We invited friends and family. A good time was had by all!

While working at the pre-school, I earned enough to buy a small life insurance policy on myself. Somehow with seven children that seemed important to me. When the school year ended, so did the job as it was a state funded school and the funds ran out. So now what? Three years at a task was about max for me anyhow, as I would start to get bored.

25th Wedding anniversary, 1979.

CHAPTER SEVEN

THE EIGHTIES

As I reflect on this decade, with all entering school and some leaving for college, I see I got extremely busy with volunteer activities. I suppose I was anxious to make new friends, having lost contact with others in moving so often, but I also needed to find a way to gain self-esteem. I served on every PTA board, from Sacred Heart to Salinas High to Palma to Notre Dame High School. I'd worked in Girl Scouts, for Bobby Sox Softball, the Salinas Area Community Chest, the Great Books Foundation, the United Way and The Central Mission Trails Heart Association. I also worked on Women's Day at Hartnell College and on Burt Talcott's campaign for the House of Representatives. I spoke at Hartnell's Child Abuse Conference on Family and at Notre Dame High's class on marriage. My advice on marriage surprises me now. "To enter marriage, you must be really alive and willing to grow." I admonished them to "be cautious in making their decision and then be reckless in living out that decision."

It still frustrated me that none of my goals as a twenty-something had been attained nor did it look like they ever would be. Somehow growing up with a dad so dedicated to educating girls and in the same era as Gloria Steinem, I was expecting great things of myself. I still wanted to teach so applied at Salinas Adult School and was hired to do what I know best—teach parents how to relate to preschoolers. The class was called

Mommy and Me and met one or two mornings a week. They brought their child to school where I had a babysitter and then worked with the parent sometimes getting a speaker to advise them. For example, a children's dentist to explain what parents can teach children about teeth care and at what age to schedule the first dental visit. Other times talking about such topics as how and when to say "No" to the child and mean it. And why! Some moms just couldn't envision denying their child anything. Explaining that setting limits for children made them feel safer. It seemed a foreign concept but I had experienced this and knew it to be true.

Somewhere in the late '70s we were asked to make a Cursillo, a three-day short course on Christianity. The men went one Thursday night to Sunday evening and the women went a couple of weekends later. Attending seemed to fit with my new understanding of how to pray. The first day was devoted to talking about God and God's love for us and the second day was about us and our love for God. The third day was about using this relationship to enable us to love our neighbor. After these weekends we divided into prayer groups of three to five couples and singles to meet regularly (bi-monthly) to pray and to share whatever was going on in our lives and to discuss how God might be speaking to us. This was helpful but also added to our already hectic schedule as the meetings rotated to each other's houses. We continued this into the '80s at which time I found a daytime scripture class called SEEK.

SEEK stands for Study, Encourage, Enrich and Kinship. This was a group of some forty women who met one morning a week for an opening talk by the leader, discussion of bible passages in small groups and a closing summary mostly emphasizing how the Spirit speaks to us through scripture. I had never really studied scripture but when the leader found I was a teacher, she encouraged me to lead one of her evening classes in the outlying parishes. She encouraged me to take a summer class at University

Isolation is greatest problem

Classes help moms and tots

By KATHLEEN MACDONALD
Californian Staff Writer

When Margaret Marcroft's oldest children were toddlers, she didn't play with them much.

She was too busy, taking care of four children under 5 years old.

Marcroft eventually had seven children and had time for fun with the younger ones.

As the years wore on, Marcroft looked back and decided that her older children had gone through fierce "terrible twos" and as teens were difficult at times to get along with.

Yet, Marcroft found that her younger children had had a much easier time of both difficult growing-up stages.

Marcroft's advice to parents is to take five minutes to toss a ball or roughhouse with their children because it can pay off in closer ties and fewer problems.

And, it is Marcroft's business to know what's good for kids and parents.

She is the instructor for Exploring Times, an eight-session program for mothers and their youngsters from 18 months to 3 years old. The program, developed three years ago, is conducted through the Salinas Adult School and is one of a series of programs designed to help parents of young children. Parents pay one $5 fee to pay for a babysitter during the sessions, but the classes are free.

From 15 to 20 mothers are in each class, usually held one morning a week for two hours.

One parent who vouches for the classes is Sue Strand. She says the classes have helped her relax.

"I probably let things ride and accept them as part of growing up more than I would have," Strand says.

The classes also helped her realize that her daughter, Jennifer, needed more time away from mom and with other kids, Strand said. They have taken the Exploring Times session twice and the first time Jennifer had a lot of trouble adjusting to all the other toddlers. A year later, she is doing much better and Strand believes the adjustment to school will be smoother when the time comes.

The sessions begin each week at the First United Methodist Church, at Lincoln Avenue and West San Luis Street, with the mothers giving their toddlers a chance to relax in the playroom. They are left there with two or more babysitters, usually Hartnell early childhood development students.

The mothers go to a nearby room to listen and talk about the topic of the day with Marcroft.

Dee Dee La Chance, who attends with son Jason, likes the discussion because it helps her think about how she acts and talks to her children.

"You don't realize how negative you can be with children until it is pointed out," she says.

At the classes, mothers talk about how to talk to children, health needs, nutrition, leisure activities with children, discipline, normal developmental changes to watch for and what makes a good toy.

"There is so much material," Marcroft said. "We pick and choose" according to the interests of the group.

Marcroft leads discussion and often brings a speaker to add expertise to the talk. There are also handouts on the subjects.

Mothers trade information about the problems they have already faced and how they solved them. And Marcroft can add her experience and her training as a teacher to the effort.

One mother told the group how she watched from the window and wept when her mother would leave her. Her daughter had recently started a repeat of the crying a generation later. How should the mother handle it?

"I got her to talk with the little girl telling her, 'You really miss me. I know you're afraid that I won't come back, but I will,'" Marcroft said.

Talking to the girl helped her, Marcroft said. Parents hesitate to talk to kids who can barely pronounce the simplest of words, but they are making a mistake.

"Many times you can see on their faces that they understand," she says. "If you leave such matters to their imagination, it takes them into more fear than if it is talked about."

Sometimes parents come up with ideas that others try.

One was leaving her child for a week to go on a trip. To fend off lonesome twinges her toddler might have, a mother taped her voice reading familiar stories to the little girl. The father taped one too.

They were played for the girl every night before bed.

(Californian photo)

Margaret Marcroft talks with other mothers.

The classes give mothers a chance to share such ideas with each other. The mothers often become friends.

Marcroft sees the classes as "a real support group for the mothers."

"I think isolation is a great problem when a woman is at home."

Marcroft tries to convey some messages to her mothers.

Some of them:

— "Children are people, too. They are individuals and not be put down because they are small in stature."

— "Keep your sense of humor through all the travail.

— Constantly evaluate how you talk to your child and how they are doing, but don't dwell on the mistakes you make as a parent.

"Take each day separately," she said. "Forget about yesterday. Learn from your mistakes and start over tomorrow."

Mommy and me class.

of San Francisco (USF) to better prepare myself. On checking it out I found the tuition exorbitant and beside I was now playing tennis on the Titus Club "C" team. We still had three in college and even though Terri and Cathy would be graduating soon, Carol and Janet would be starting and Lisa would be in Notre Dame, a private high school. After checking out the cost, I shelved the whole idea.

All through the early 1980s I continued to teach and counsel young parents in the Mommy and Me classes, I also established a TV program run out of the Monterey District Office of Education, which we dubbed "In Our Footsteps." We did weekly shows from September 1981 to June 1982 in which we showed a film and then I led a group discussion with locals who had some experience with the topic. The locals were contacted by my helper, Kathy D. who also provided me with a children's book or recipe to suggest for use by the parents watching. The show was aired on the local channel three times a week, morning, afternoon (4:30) and 7 in the evening and the topics ranged from how to talk to preschoolers and young children about moving, parental divorce, losing a grandparent, food allergies, play-ground manners, sibling rivalry, etc. It was great fun and our only disappointment was we were not picked up by any national network.

Between the late '70s and through 1982 I continued to visit Mom at the convalescent hospital almost daily, take Mrs. Thompson (our adopted grandmother and neighbor from our two years on Riker Street) shopping weekly as well as weekly bible study, tennis and dance lessons plus handling the banking for John's business and going to games to see the girls play sports. Dinner and the wash became just automatic. Somehow in November 1981 we managed a week in Acapulco with our friends the Kruse's.

Early in Easter week of 1982 Katherine Convalescent called to say Mom definitely was not doing well. Ed and I, Janet and Lisa went over right

My mom and my siblings.

after dinner; leaving a note for Carol to join us as soon as she got home. She did and we sat around Mom's bed and said the rosary, taking turns leading a decade. I could see Mom smile, hearing her favorite prayer, and as we finished the nurse came in and said we may as well go home as it could be up to 24 hrs. We no sooner got into bed than the nurse phoned and said Mom had died. Her funeral was scheduled for the first Wednesday in April 1982 in Exeter, California and she was buried in Visalia the next day. All the children were there and all my siblings. Our neighbors from the Santa Monica Way potluck group, Tom and Linda, were there, a large group from the Catholic Daughters of America, for whom Mom had worked so hard, was also present as well as most of Mom's twenty-five grandchildren. It was a grand send off!

At the ranch after Mom's funeral.

The four younger girls all liked their sports; most being three sport people during high school. Our oldest girl, Cathy was into drama and plays as an extra-curricular activity, Mike played football and Terri spent time on the debate team and at math contests after school. During the summer Carol liked to go to Hartnell for pickup volleyball games when she was home from Fresno State. One evening Mike, who had been living on his own and had not met our new neighbor, Tom, was over for dinner and answered the door. Tom frequently drove Carol to Hartnell as they both liked volleyball and it gave him a break from his two little girls. No sense taking two cars when they lived next door. Ever protective big brother Mike thought Tom a bit old to date Carol and said so. Fortunately, Carol came up to explain the situation. Tom also had to insist Carol call him "Tom" not "Mr. W." as that made him feel too old.

1982 was a sad year! Not only did we lose Mom but also that fall our beloved neighbor, Jack of Jack and Betty, one of the potluck six couples, took sick with pancreatic cancer, suffering through most of 1983 and dying early 1984. Jack was our age and had a terrific sense of humor. His wife Betty and I took belly dancing lessons for a few months so for Christmas he gave us each a "jewel" for our navel. Also, our adopted grandmother Mrs. Thompson passed away in Wisconsin in August of 1982. Her granddaughter had come in October 1981 and moved her back east where all her family lived. This was a relief for me as by then she could not drive and I was running errands for her.

The school year of '82–'83 brought a whole new kind of change. Lisa was a senior in high school and was looking forward to being the only one home and having the "kid's" car to herself. In September we loaded up that car and mine and all four of us started out to deliver Janet to Cal Poly, her choice of higher education, wanting to follow in her Grandpa's footsteps. Half way to San Luis Obispo, a large piece of metal flew off a flatbed truck going north which careened across the center divider and hit Janet's car post right behind the driver bending it into a V and breaking all the glass on that side of the car. The girls pulled over and we drove up right behind them. So scary! Lisa was angry that she couldn't have the car 'till it was fixed.

On top of that I'd been asked to take in a senior girl, (since we had this big mostly empty house) as a boarder for the year. Ellen, the youngest of ten, went home on Fridays to her widower father and came back Sunday nights. By October the car was back and Lisa was happy again. The one thing that bothered me was that with two phone lines in the house, the two girls would each get one and stay on the phone for hours. One night when John was out of town and I was at a meeting I had tried to call home to see if John had left a message but after several tries when I could not get through, I just drove home to find a girl on each a phone. I berated both of them saying the phone was not a toy and they needed to leave sometime between calls so someone could call in. Then I sent them to bed. Some twenty years later, I ran into Ellen one evening in Monterey at a live theater performance. During intermission we had a mini-reunion. She told me she had always wanted to thank me for that year as I was the only person she could remember "who cared enough for her to set limits." I was flabbergasted as all I could think of was the night I lost my cool with the girls.

Meantime, Janet was finding her chosen major at Cal Poly was not for her, but Cal Poly did not allow students to switch majors midyear, so come winter, she transferred to San Diego State to try out Graphic Design, her new choice. She liked the major but the house mates proved to be anything but congenial. We spent lots of time on the phone. It was decided she would go to Hartnell her sophomore year and live at home, then transfer back into Cal Poly. Lisa also decided to go to Hartnell as a freshman. She said she'd had so much fun as a high school senior she hadn't had time to apply to a four-year college (and I did not do applications). In '83-'84 through our parish, Sacred Heart, we were again asked to take in a boarder for one year, this time a Hartnell student from Brazil who needed to learn English. Fran had a hard time at first as she was so homesick and on weekends spent her time at the convent with her aunt, who was a nun. She gradually adjusted and began spending weekends at our house and the three girls went to dances and school activities together. She ever after claimed to have been adopted.

Fran Marques.

What I found hard to believe was that neither of these girls had ever had a party given in their honor till a birthday party at our house. We let them invite whom they pleased, choose the menu and in general be the guest of honor. Lots of tears of joy! Both Ellen and Fran have become contributing members of society.

For two years, September '83 to June '85, during the school year I worked in our local parish as ministry coordinator, still teaching parenting, this time to Sacred Heart parents at night using the programs, Focus on The Family and Parent Effectiveness Training or PET. These demands on my time seemed to form a framework within which I could exist while my older four children were flying the coop. Maybe it was stated, don't remember, that Dad and I only paid for the first (bachelor) degree; any other degree was on them. Terri graduated Santa Clara June '80 and went to work in San Jose for a couple of years. Cathy finished Long Beach in December '81, but walked in May '82. That fall Cathy left for a masters program on a full scholarship to Cornell University in New York while Terri left for Phoenix, Arizona to attend Thunderbird School of Global Management where she became fluent in German and got her Masters in International Management (with honors) on her own.

In early summer of '83, Mike struck out on a course of higher learning of a different kind when he quit his job, bought a VW van and started to visit as many states and cousins as he could. Occasionally he had to stop and work a spell but he travelled from early June to Thanksgiving that year seeing some forty-seven of the fifty states. Joan had transferred to Colorado State from Hartnell, so Mike got to visit his three sisters in the

189

cities of Phoenix, AZ, Loveland, CO and Ithaca, NY. He called home after each visit to say how the girls and he had spent their time. Ed and I met him in Phoenix as Terri was graduating that summer, August 1983.

Carol, the oldest of the three youngest girls graduated Notre Dame High School in June '81 and was off to Fresno State that year. She had two years done when the older four started their traveling around; she continued to come home summers.

In the spring of '83 I had been talking to USF about their four-summer course on Spirituality, a master's program called Master in Applied Spirituality (MAS). The program consisted of three summers of six weeks of course work and one summer of a thirty-day silent retreat called the Spiritual Exercises of St. Ignatius. For the three summers I could go to San Francisco on Sunday night and return on Friday afternoon but the second summer, for the retreat, I could not come home at all. As I said earlier, the cost was exorbitant and so I'd dismissed the idea.

Two weeks after I'd talked to the school, my brother called and said the folks' estate had settled and I would be getting exactly the cost I needed for the next four summers. Fate? Not likely, more probably an answer to prayer. So, I talked it over with the three younger girls and my husband. None were too excited about it but Carol and Janet each always had summer jobs and John's work kept him away a lot. Since Lisa didn't see a need to work, she was elected to cook the evening meal each day Monday through Friday and do the laundry for all at home. We would make out the menu on Saturdays and grocery shop for the week. The second summer while I was gone five-six weeks was the toughest on all of them, especially Carol who had to pay the bills and see that the cars were running. Lisa did get a job and had summer work from then on. I, on the other hand, had time with other adults, myself and my God. It proved to be life-giving and nothing drastic happened at home. My husband did get a lot of things fixed and remodeled my kitchen with a small inheritance he received while I was gone. All seemed happy to have me home.

During the third summer, I was asked to write a paper for my class on Shared Ministry for which I drew heavily from my job at Sacred Heart. After Vatican II I found it more acceptable to work in the Church, though I was still somewhat ambivalent. Having separated my God from my church and having a Jesuit professor explain that religions were meant to be a "finger pointing to the moon"; in other words our religion is a guide to our God, not a be all and end all in itself, I felt less troubled by my reservations about the Catholic Church. This understanding was to be tested many times in my future. Up to this point my ego was salved by a booklet I'd come across called "Prayer of Liberated Women" by Patricia B. Driscoll, A Christian Womanity Publication; c. 1975 St. John's International Alliance, United Kingdom and Ireland Section. It starts out "Almighty God & Savior. We proclaim your greatness. We thank you for all creation. We thank you for making Male and Female in your own image and EQUAL in your sight." The EQUAL part was important to me.

At the end of July, 1986 I graduated after giving the class speech and Mike and Joan were both engaged to be married. Janet was back at Cal Poly and Lisa was going off to Chico State. Carol had graduated Fresno State in Occupational Therapy and was working at Agnews State Hospital. Now we had three Masters in the family; Cathy in Theatre Arts, Terri in International Management and me in Applied Spirituality.

During the school years of '82 to '86, I continued to play tennis and go to Liturgical dance. At some point our dance group put on a performance called *Tales of Wonder*, staging it in various parishes in the diocese. The story is the creation story of Genesis. It was a full-on performance with

Tales of Wonder, liturgical dance.

music, lighting, costumes and participants of all ages, boys and girls, men and women. It was the culmination of years of practice and signaled the end of dance for most of us. As Cursillo required members to participate in putting on weekends for new recruits, we did our share, working several weekends from the late '70s to the late '80s, either giving inspirational talks and being discussion leaders or cooking for a group of about fifty, more or less. I opted not to COOK! Cursillo continued to feed me spiritually. One of my talks was based on equality using a holy card I had been given with only the word "Jesus" written in bold red lines.

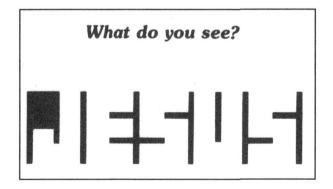

What do you see?

Glancing quickly at this card, one might not see a word at all; only lines and spaces. I told the women one interpretation was the straight lines were male as truthful God-fearing men could be pretty rigid in their efforts to follow "the rule of God's law." I felt the spaces between the lines were female; also believing, God–loving people who tended to follow the "spirit of God's law." Both were needed to make any sense of this journey through this world, to be happy with God in the next. God had planned for us to follow Jesus back to the Creator. Some women have a stronger sense of the law than others and some men have a stronger sense of the spirit but both are absolutely needed in equal parts to fulfill God's plan. I wasn't trying to establish new theology but rather wanting to give people a visual with which to relate.

I also continued bible study on Tuesday mornings and started leading a class at the Madonna Del Sasso Parish which I did one night a week for almost ten school years. In late 1986 we changed parishes and began attending St. Joseph's in Spreckels.

One Sunday that fall I decided to give a dinner party for us and three other couples. I know we had agreed on a date but as I was fixing dinner John came downstairs with his travel bag all packed. I asked him where he was going and he said he had a 2 p.m. plane to catch. It was definitely too late to call off the guests so the seven of us had a great dinner and visit much to my embarrassment. One of the guests suggested each couple and myself write John a "thank you" telling him thank you for the use of his house and how much he was missed. They came in the mail but he never acknowledged them. That's how busy he was and how well his business was going. He had switched his emphasis from walking fields looking for insects to crop loss investigating and occasionally testifying in court as an expert witness. We incorporated the business and established a retirement fund for us and any employees and had begun investing in an old home which he remodeled for his office, but we needed a financial planner and went through two in the next few years before we found an honest one; a costly learning curve for us!

Upon graduating from University of San Francisco, we were into the wedding scene, which lasted from August 1986 to December 1995. Mike had decided on a Salinas native, Debbie Kaslin, a girl who had been in my Girl Scout troop and that we already loved. They picked August 9th for the wedding, as that was the only date they could get both the church and the reception hall they wanted on the same day in August. Unfortunately, Cathy had signed an acting contract in the Midwest through August 16th, which meant she couldn't get home for the wedding. That seemed to be the one hitch in the event. Mike eased that pain for Cathy by sending her flowers, very sweet.

Once the dam was broken, there was to be a wedding every year between our children and my brother Vince and sister Fran's children, for the next ten years. We attended all of them, of course, and I loved seeing so much more of my brothers and sisters.

Joan and Pete decided 1986 was also their year, arranging their wedding in Salinas from Loveland, CO, which proved to be a bit of a challenge. It was finally set for December 31, '86 at Sacred Heart Church followed by a reception in Monterey with a band that would see us into the New Year. Looking back that did seem typically Joan! Swiftly following were Carol, Cathy, Lisa, Janet and Terri. A year or two later, I found that between bridesmaid dresses and prom dresses one whole closet was full! I set about finding somewhere to donate them.

Mike's wedding, August 9, 1986.

Joan's wedding, December 31, 1986; me, Fran, Dorothy and Elizabeth.

Grandparents—Who are They?

Where we grew up, five miles from town with only one car, most of the people I saw were my age, my siblings' ages or that of my parents. One grandmother lived with us for only a summer as Dad was her oldest son but she soon became so ill she moved into town and lived with her two daughters, my aunts. While she was with us, I do remember taking breakfast on a tray to the bedroom for her then plopping into bed with her and eating it. She was happy for the company and didn't feel like eating anyway. When I went to visit her in town, she always had a holy card to give me. There are only three in my scrap book, but she gave me many. She died when I was about eight of bone cancer.

My other grandparent was Mom's dad who made soap in the backyard with the fat renderings from the pig Dad butchered every year. He used lye and chunks of fat that he stirred with a long stick in a huge black caldron over an open fire. We were cautioned to stand "way back" because the lye burned if it splashed on your skin. The end product looked something like Fels-Naptha bars. He too lived with us for a short time but as his health deteriorated, it became necessary for the folks to move him to the Old People's Home in town.

I guess the closest model we had of a grandparent was Frank, the man who came to dinner and stayed eight years more or less,

He bought us treats and sat and talked to us in his broken Sicilian accent and always laughed at our antics. His laugh was magical.

When my own children came along, Mom and Dad were very good grandparents, always welcoming at holidays and in the summer when we would take the children to the ranch for a week to just get warm, swim in the "ditches" as I had, and just feel the joy of open space. The ranch was a place to play with cousins, eat watermelons till you almost burst, and listen to the frogs at night under the clear night sky ablaze with stars.

My children's memories of grandparents may have extended into their teen years for by the time Cathy, our oldest was 17 only my mother was living and she had Alzheimer's disease so a real relationship was impossible. In 1968 my husband's mother died and his dad remarried two and a half years later. Bernice was the epitome of a wonderful mother-in-law and grandmother. Even though John's dad died just two years after they married, she remembered every birthday of our seven children for the next twenty-five years. She even volunteered to spend a week with the children ranging then from eight to eighteen while we took a much-needed vacation. She shuttled kids to events as necessary and made sure the older ones reported in every night. Our oldest had moved out and our second was at Hartnell. There were two girls in high school and three in grade school. We heard funny stories when we got home but all were safe and I was so grateful I couldn't thank her enough. Bernice was probably the grandmother the children knew best. She was also the grandmother present at all their weddings and attended our first grandchild's first birthday.

The other grandmother was one we adopted, named Teresa Thompson. We met her in Salinas where our 6th child was born in the spring of '65. She was the caregiver for the 90-year-old lady next door. About once a month she would phone just after dinner

Bernice with Emma and Cathy.

Mrs. Thompson with Carol.

and ask for John's help. Her 90 year old charge, about six feet tall, would throw herself on the floor and Teresa (5 X 5) needed my husband to help lift her back into bed. She'd come for dinner for all the children's birthdays during our 20-month stay and always gave each child a quarter, much to their delight. When we moved to Fresno, she kept tabs on us and when our 7th child was born, she drove over to see us and at least once I drove the children on a Saturday to the top of Pacheco Pass and she met us there for a picnic lunch. After twenty months we moved back to Salinas, by then she was living in a mobile home park by herself. She became a regular visitor for holidays and birthdays. Mrs. Thompson's favorite way of greeting the girls was by asking each one, "How's your love life?" This caused the girls great dismay; they weren't really going to tell her but then, how to be polite? Her family all lived in Wisconsin. Every September till she was 90 she drove back to spend that month with her own grandchildren. For the next three years I took her to S.F. airport and picked her up a month later. When she became too disabled to live alone they sent a granddaughter to come move her to Wisconsin. Upon her arrival they put her in a nursing home. I was livid!

The last and funniest memory of Teresa and my mom occurred at Christmas, '80. John's childless Aunt Hildur recently widowed and in her 80s decided to fly out from Minnesota for Christmas. Though very deaf, she had carefully packed her hearing aids in her checked luggage. When she didn't show at Monterey airport, John had the airlines check and "yes she had gotten to San Francisco" but never answered a page. Finally, on the third commuter plane she arrived and John, in exasperation said "I was so worried! We didn't know where you were." She replied calmly, "God knew where I was." To which John replied, "Well, He didn't tell me!"

The next day was Christmas and Teresa Thompson drove

over to our house, but the children had to help her out of her car and up the three steps into the house as her knees were giving out under her weight. Our older girls fetched my mother from Katherine Convalescent Hospital where she resided as her Alzheimer's advanced. I spaced the children between the older women around the table—one who could converse but not reach or walk far, one who could walk but not hear and my mom who was physically quick but mindless. The meal erupted in chaos as Mom who couldn't ask for food to be passed and couldn't be heard by Hildur anyway and was too far from Teresa's short reach suddenly used her fork to spear food from any plate she chose, much to the children's shock as they were saving that precious bite of pineapple (or whatever) for the last. Laughter saved the day as I raced around the table to help Mom to seconds and reminded the children Grandma just didn't know what she was doing.

So, one takes "grandparents" where you can find them and appreciates the love they exhibit, regardless of the circumstances.

LATE EIGHTIES

Two more weddings followed in the late eighties, Carol's and Cathy's. In the meantime, I worked on a committee of women to respond to a midwestern bishop, Bishop Imesch's questionnaire about Women in the Catholic Church. His idea was to compile our answers into a Pastoral Letter to the other bishops in the United States regarding women's contributions and our standing in our church, whether to allow altar girls, women deacons, etc. The project became over-whelming apparently, as a Pastoral Letter never appeared. We did begin to see altar girls ten years later but so far, no women deacons.

In late '86 I also began a program, R.C.I.A. (Right of Christian Initiation of Adults) in my new parish for people who wanted to study and join the Catholic Church. I did this for three years. I had sponsored my friend Barbara K. three years before when she joined the Catholic Church. At the same time in my zeal for teaching and the church I co-taught, with priests, evening classes to adults for the Monterey Diocesan School of Ministry. Fr. Mike and I alternated going to San Luis Obispo to teach weekly. It seems one participant had not read the brochure correctly and when I showed up the second week, he wanted to know where Fr. Mike was. When I explained our format, that I would teach every other week, he gave me a five-minute dressing down; Fr. Mike was supposed to come every week. When he finished, I resumed class and did not refer to his remarks again. He kept coming for some reason. These people were being

Me and Barbara.

prepared to become lectors and eucharistic ministers (new lay positions in the church) to help the priests. There now were an increased number of churchgoers just as the number of priests dwindled.

As time progressed the diocese saw fit to buy more property in Monterey so funds for the school ran out. Still I had hopes of making a difference in the relationship between clergy and laity so when the bishop asked me to work with Fr. Larry to form a Diocesan Pastoral Council, I happily traveled to the forty-five parishes in our diocese to explain and cajole. The idea was to get three representatives from each parish to then form a board who would advise the bishop on any needs or gifts available within the ranks of the laity for his consultation. After three years and much travel and many meetings we had a solid organization formed — at which point the bishop died and the new bishop saw no need for Diocesan Council.

I finally got the message and went to work on the board of The Catholic Women's Network, a newspaper out of Sunnyvale, which I distributed and wrote for. Arlene Goetze, the editor had founded it to support women like me who had worked for the church but were faceless. This kept me busy from January '88 to December '04. We on the board put on workshops and wrote entries for the two inspirational books Arlene compiled. Both the books and all 89 issues of the newspaper are stored in the University of Santa Clara Library Archives. During these years I used the paper to advertise my women's retreats given at St. Francis Retreat Center in San Juan Bautista during '94, '95 and '96. At one of these gatherings the women decorated and sewed together quilt squares leaving me with a beautiful memento.

But I'm getting ahead of the story. In June of 1987 University of San Francisco hired Fr. Kevin Feeney and me to come back to campus as Spiritual Directors and to work with the graduating class. We met individually with students, attended some workshops, planned liturgies, gave reflections or homilies and generally spent time with the class of '87. I was going back and forth to Salinas to prepare for Carol's wedding shower and wedding, August 22nd. To top it all off, our dear friends from Watsonville days lost one of their four sons, Mark, to AIDS in July in San Francisco. John and I attended the funeral and seeing Jolly and Dulce was heart breaking. He had been such a pistol! I could still remember the day I returned the four boys to Dulce after babysitting them and breaking into tears as I had to tell her I had given Mark a hard swat for disobeying me. When I told her the circumstances, she said she would have done the same thing! I felt a bit better after that. Even more sad, Dulce and Jolly also lost their oldest that following December also to AIDS. That left just two boys instead of four!

In '89 John and I took our first cruise up the inland passage of Alaska for a week. I delighted in not cooking and getting dressed up every night for dinner. Being an introvert, Ed was happy to be seated at a table for two, but I craved more people so we eventually joined a table of six. It seemed I was not used to only having two of the children home and seeing fewer adults in the summer, as I was not at USF anymore.

In June of 1988 Janet graduated from Cal Poly, then in the fall of 1988 our first grandchild was born on September 27th. Timothy was a delight from the start; a real people person. We usually had Christmas at our house and having a baby present changed everything. The following April 1st Cathy and Will got married just before our 35th anniversary on June 26, 1989. To celebrate that occasion the plan was for Mike and Debbie to take us to the wharf for a late lunch after Timothy's nap. We went to their house to wait for him to wake up and when he did, we stopped at our house to drop him off with Carol, Janet and Lisa. I was carrying him in and I as I got to the family room I glanced to my left and saw a whole room full of people, if Debbie hadn't rushed forward, I might have dropped Timothy, I was so surprised. The party was truly a welcome surprise! Mike had loaded his car with meat to bar-b-que and the girls had made salads. They provided a grand meal for our friends. With John's business going full tilt and me working for the church and on weddings, it had been hard. That evening I remember agreeing to reset and start again.

Besides all this we had bought and sold (just breaking even), not one but two properties in Arroyo Seco, trying to find a warm place to spend summers. But with John unable to be with us, I felt the responsibility of teenage kids and their friends to be too much, so we abandoned the idea.

We were still very involved with Cursillo which was a blessing mostly but took a lot of time. In October of '89 we agreed to keep Timothy for a weekend as his parents went to a produce convention. That was fun. Janet and I took him to the park and generally played with him all weekend. He was good-natured but was so glad to see his parents back!!! The love was palpable.

Timothy.

October 15, 1989—Timothy at One

"Unless you become as little children,
you shall not enter the kingdom of heaven." (Matthew 18:3)

What does it mean?

I received a real insight into this scripture when our son and his wife went out of town on a Friday morning leaving their 13-month-old son with his aunt and uncle for 24 hours. Then on Saturday morning I brought him to our house, to grandmother's. He was cheerful and accepting of all the change—new surroundings, new bed, new caretakers. In his accepting good humor he was a total delight. He rejoiced while crawling around the house investigating a "new place"; was happy to be strolled through a different neighborhood to a park not familiar to him. He had a good time in the swing with his aunt pushing him. When Timothy was hungry we fed him, when sleepy we put him to bed. He pulled up and walked around the furniture and threw himself down on a stack of pillows. He crawled over and rough-housed with whomever got down on the floor with him. He laughed with delight at his bath or when having his diaper changed. All in all his kisses and patty-cakes, smiles and deep-seated laughter enriched my weekend beyond measure. There was no sadness or unhappiness in him and he seemed not even to notice his mother and father were gone.

Then Sunday about 5:45 pm they returned. He'd just finished dinner and was still in his chair. He looked toward the front door when he heard their voices and laughed out loud as his mom and dad rounded the corner into the kitchen. Then two seconds of absolute silence were followed by heart breaking sobs—gut wrenching, unstoppable sobs. They had come back for him!

And I ask myself, "Is that how it will be with us—me when I finally see God?" If so, then does Scripture ask me to be just as accepting and obedient, joyful and loving of others while I'm here on earth as Timothy was while at my house? He knew, at thirteen months, that it was those two special people he needed and wanted most in his life. Only they could make his life complete no matter how well I'd cared for him.

Jesus, when I see you face to face on that new day, will I understand as Timothy did that no matter how well the world treats me there will always be something missing until I'm with you; not just something but the most important thing. If that's how it will be then please God, keep this image of an obedient, contented, joy-filled child before me as a constant model. Do I enrich God's world by just being here? Do I accept the care I get from others even if it is often inadequate in my mind—not as kind and merciful as I'd like? Can I wait with patience until God comes for me in God's time? If so, I may have learned a bit of what children already know. I was a child once. Help me to remember what is deep in my unconscious.

Timothy's equanimity seemed restored after a short period of being held close by each parent. He then could show off for them and even go on about his business of crawling and investigating with perfect aplomb. All was right with his world again.

Occasionally we also suddenly recognize that a great chasm has opened between us and our God. Ironically it is not God who went away but we who distance ourselves by not acting in love. When we realize this we have only to cry out and God will hold us close wrapped in grace till we can again continue our journey toward the kingdom.

CHAPTER 8—PART 1

THE NINETIES

In the '80s I really concentrated on growing intellectually and spiritually as well as keeping up the physical activity. I got on a tennis team that competed both in Santa Cruz and Monterey counties. Great fun!

I went along with the flow of college graduations and weddings and children striking out on their own; going to live in New York or getting a job in Austria or starting a family. Suddenly I realized I had not processed my feelings at all, I was just stuffing them! As I started to unpack them, I saw I was letting myself get fearful about things I could not control. A friend told me FEAR stands for Fantasized Experiences Appearing Real. The definition still works today. I've worked hard to not let fear become a way of coping, making decisions, or of going forward. I also found I was dreaming excessively so started recording them and working with a dream analyst. She helped me see I was processing through dreams what I was stuffing and not dealing with. All this led to reading a lot of Carl Jung's books and quite a few books of my recorded dreams are gathering dust in the closet. I needed to keep moving. I had my colors done, found I was a "winter" (not a surprise) and then gave myself a modeling class as a sixtieth birthday present. Maybe I just needed a bit of sprucing up!

By now I was really tired of the wind and fog of Salinas and could see the sun out in the canyon from our family room window. Our friends,

Jack and Starr, next door had been transferred away by Firestone and the new neighbor was most unpleasant. My knee started acting up as most of my girls were gone, and they'd always helped me clean and carry laundry back upstairs. I started looking for a one-story house out in the canyon. I found one in The Meadows and started cleaning out twenty-five years of living at Santa Monica Way. Since it took awhile to sell our house in town, I had time to go room-by-room and pack up what we wanted to take. On the last day, Mike came over and helped me pack up the kitchen after dinner. He wanted to say good-by to the house as well. I came back a couple of days later and video-taped all the house really half wishing we had kept it as I remembered all the good times we'd had there. So glad I have the video on disc now to relive the good times as well as some of the hard times!

The grandbabies started coming in '90 as Paul joined Timothy, Mike and Debbie, and Emma joined Cathy and Will in Chicago right after Thanksgiving. Three more weddings followed in the first half of the nineties. Lisa and Rich married in January 1992 and we moved out of our big house to the sun belt in May. Janet and Jim married in December 1993 and Jim brought with him Jake, seven and Tess five. Terri and Dave married in late 1995. By then Joan and Pete had moved to Reno and Maureen arrived a year after Emma almost to the day. Marina followed in March 1993 to Carol and Brendan, then living in Texas. John and I were getting to see country we'd never seen before. Steven joined Timothy and Paul in May '93 bringing our total number of grandchildren to eight by December 1993. The bumper year was October, 1994 to October, 1995 during which we received four grandsons in twelve months — Mason to Lisa and Rich, Ross to Joan and Pete, Collin to Carol and Brendan and Peter to Cathy and Will! All big healthy babies arriving within twelve months! Lots of babies at Terri and Dave's wedding that December; Peter was just seven weeks old! Now, we had twelve — eight boys and four girls. All evened out with four more girls joining us in the next few years — Katrina to Lisa and Rich, Rebecca to Janet and Jim, Sydney to Terri and Dave and Justine to Janet and Jim.

Moving to a new community brought different challenges - getting to know people in the new neighborhood and how the gated community worked. There were quite a few people in our age group who did a lot of traveling so for several falls I invited six or eight couples to the back deck to talk about their most recent travels and have a glass of wine. The more we learned about our gated community, the more we understood it is run by a board of residents. We soon found ourselves on the board; John as Landscape Chairman and me as a board member for two years then President of the board for two. During that time the bridge washed out during a rainy winter in the late '90s so I was quite busy meeting with engineers, etc. I also joined the local tennis club, Chamisal. My partner, Marilyn and I were getting better.

In 1994 John decided to sell his business as he was lucky enough to find a buyer; he wanted to spend more time with the grandchildren who were growing "like weeds" as the saying goes. Though he sold in 1994, it took him three to four years to close all his cases. In the meantime, he rented the building to the new owner, Dale.

The children were starting to take their kids camping and as Debbie's family had always camped at Pinecrest (Strawberry) Lake, they gathered there. Joan and Pete had moved to New Jersey so in 1997 we rented a cabin near the campground so she and kids could fly out and stay with us, play at the lake and go to campfires with cousins. While there, John found a cabin he liked and told us he had spent time on this lake as a teen. We even found pictures so know it's true. Before you could count to ten, John made

Marcroft Manor at Pinecrest.

an offer on the cabin and put his Salinas office up for sale. The girls were glad as they'd been doing the janitorial duties, Jan and a friend had even painted the whole outside for spending money during their teen years. We have spent the week between Christmas and New Year's at the cabin, in the snow with many families for many years starting in 1997. The first year brought one-month-old Rebecca in a swing at the sliding glass door mesmerized by the white stuff outside. In these past 23 years the tri-level, four-car garage, three bath, four bedroom plus den house has seen a lot of living!

The 1990s also brought some travel for John and me. He particularly liked to travel and I just wanted to keep up with friends. Unfortunately, my first trip was to Seattle to help my sister Eileen when her husband, Jim, died unexpectedly in September, it was the start of a hard time for her. We were fortunate to have the money so between baptisms and first

John and I with Jolly (third from right) and Dulce (second from right).

communions we did get to do some adventuresome travel.

In January 1993 we were invited to go on a three-day cruise to celebrate our friends' 40th anniversary. We had known Jolly and Dulce all but five of those 40 years. One of the pluses of buying the cabin was its proximity to these two. The night before the cruise ended, we were to have our luggage packed and out in the hall by midnight. Ed and Dulce had picked up some kind of stomach bug so I packed John's bag and Jolly packed Dulce's. I did such a good job that John had no shirt to wear the next morning and had to go to breakfast in pants and jacket. All had a great laugh!

Speaking of keeping up with old friends, the next November we took a Tauck Tour to Australia-New Zealand with the Franeys, Elinor, I'd known since grammar school and Roger I met when they married. They had raised eight children and we seven, just spending weekends together a couple of times, so I guess we felt we needed a three-week no holds barred trip. It was great but we missed Thanksgiving with the family. We did talk on the phone but that's hardly the same.

April 1995 saw us going to the San Blas islands and through the Panama Canal with Bob and Sue, our friends from Chualar reminiscing about old times at their swimming pool on the ranch in the '60s and many more get-togethers in the '70s and '80s. We enjoyed Stanford-San Jose State football games every fall with elaborate tailgate parties, silver candle sticks etc. (Sue was definitely the "hostess with the mostess") and attending all our children's weddings. By now we were both "empty nesters." Along the line Ed started collecting a plate from each country we visited, so now plates line our family room walls!!!

In January 1996, just as Ed was nearing retirement, Western Farm Service engaged him to give a seminar to their men while on a trip to Cabo San Lucas. This was great fun! Ed got to do his first parasailing (as I had done in '75) the timing of which made us miss the departure of the dinner cruise. We had to catch up via a water taxi and a rope ladder (while in white slacks). Lots of laughs all around!!

In June of '96 we went to the United Kingdom after a week in Ireland on a tour organized by Frank and Mary Beth Byrnes which included lots of fellow parishioners from St. Joseph's as well as Fr. Patrick Dooling and Fr. Mike Miller. There was so much to see and somehow it felt like home. After the tour departed, we stayed on a few days with Mike and Marilyn, my tennis doubles partner. We rented a car and agreed Ed should drive as the Irish drove on the left side and he was left-handed. With three of us directing him it was quite hilarious. Fresh out of the airport, we couldn't get off the round-about (our first experience) until some kind Irishman noticing us going round the third time shouted "Ere ye lost?" We had

Cabo water taxi, 1996.

pulled to the side and he literally led us the first few miles toward Dublin. But the weirdest experience was turning the car in at the dock where we wanted to catch a ferry to Wales. We were in the line to board and couldn't find where to return the car. The official became exasperated with us as we were holding up the line. When John asked where to park, he said, "just dump it!" and "put the keys in the box on that building." No papers to sign or other formalities. Even so we had to run to catch the ferry. The ferry put us in Wales where we spent two over nights with nun friends from USF days in the '80s. We got royal treatment as well as our laundry done. We left there for an arranged two-week tour of Wales, Scotland and England. When we finally got home, we had been gone almost five weeks and decided that was a bit too long!

On our way to top of Half Dome, me, Mike, Janet and Carol.

In 1997 we went to Puerto Vallarta with a group from Chamisal and Mike and Marilyn for a little tennis, a little swimming, mostly relaxing. 1998 was about conditioning as John had read about some fellow who had walked across England and wanted us to do that too. For getting in shape our son, Mike took two of his sisters and us up Half Dome and back in one day, August 8, 1998. Janet was still nursing her Rebecca who stayed home with her dad so at the top she expressed the extra milk and threw it over the edge while Carol blew bubbles from a jar into space. It was dizzying to be up so high! A few weeks later it was with a feeling of accomplishment that I viewed others on top the rock as we flew back to San Francisco from England.

Our walk across England took two weeks, averaging fifteen miles per day. We started one day, mid-September at Robin Hood's Bay on the North Sea and ended at Saint Bees Head on the Irish Sea one afternoon early October. We'd left the states a couple of days early as I wanted to first stop off in Norwich, the birth place of Julian of Norwich, she is noted as having twenty-three apparitions of Christ and experiencing some of his sufferings. His final words to her though were "All will be well, all shall be well, and all manner of things shall be well!" When she questioned Him regarding all the suffering in the world, He said to trust his message. Again, in this day and age, we will do well to follow His advice. Julian also admonishes us with this quote: "…we need to fall, and

John and I on the edge.

Lunch at Hadrian's Wall, halfway across England.

we need to be aware of it; for if we did not fall we should not know how weak and wretched we are of ourselves, nor should we know our Maker's marvelous love so fully..."

The actual walk is well documented in Ed's journal and magically had only one day of rain. Our group consisted of our guide, Terry, a retired restaurateur, Chris from San Diego, a single man and two of us couples. The other couple said they regularly hiked the Appalachian Trail on the east coast; they were a retired psychiatrist, Tony, and his wife, Barbara. I found the first two days of walking through sheep pastures just boring (I did that as a child on the ranch). I quickly took to bringing up the rear and singing my way across England. I was currently in the church choir and a seniors' chorus at home. As we neared the end of the trek, I found my

Senior Singers tune up for Salinas performances

BY DAVE NORDSTRAND
dnordstrand@thecalifornian.com

Tunes evoking Broadway's bright lights, the grandness of America and even heaven's golden glow spill out the open church door.

It's the weekly rehearsal of The Senior Singers, a toe-tapping session during which some of the finest music in the universe is given its due.

"Great music, but nothing too heavy," said Joyce Solazzi, the group's director.

Solazzi took up her stance before a graying but spirited and very melodic group of 47 vocalists ages 60 to 90-plus.

Each Monday for two hours, the singers tune up their repertoire at Northminster Presbyterian Church, 315 East Alvin Drive in Salinas.

"We consider ourselves an outreach to the church," said Solazzi, 76.

"So many places would like us to come and sing. These people, even though they seem old, have wonderful energy."

The Senior Singers began its musical voyage 20 strong a decade ago as Northminster's senior choir.

The group grew in number and expanded its repertoire.

They sing in churches. They sing in nursing homes and retirement facilities.

See **SINGERS**, 3B

RICHARD GREEN/THE SALINAS CALIFORNIAN

Margaret Marcroft rehearses along with other members of The Senior Singers.

DETAILS ABOUT THE SENIOR SINGERS

The next Senior Singers concert open to the general public is at 2:30 p.m. May 24 at the Lutheran Church of the Good Shepherd, 580 Larkin St., Salinas.

The Senior Singers do not charge for their perform-

ances but do accept donations.

Anyone wishing to book the group or anyone interested in joining the singers can call Joyce Solazzi, director, at 424-3644.

Senior Singers.

pants were harder to button. One evening I complained, "How could one walk 15 to 20 miles a day and gain weight?" Barbara quickly noted that if I didn't have half a pint before dinner each night, I wouldn't gain weight. To which I replied, "If I didn't have half a pint each night I would have gone home long ago." When we stopped in New Jersey to visit Joan on our trip home, I weighed myself and quickly bought the next larger size pants for the trip home. I had gained twelve pounds walking 192 miles!!

Trying to be pious, Dorothy, me, Elizabeth and Eileen.

In the summer of '99 three of my four sisters and I decided now was the time to visit Ireland together as we knew our parents could trace relatives back to County Mayo and County Cork. John decided he needed to go to Ireland to hike with our guide, Terry, from England's walk and would meet us in Dublin after our tour and his hike. I had not had much time for my sisters in recent years and they lived in different states, Washington, Arizona, Indiana and me in California. Meeting in the Chicago airport, our flight to Ireland started with hysterical laughter—just thinking we would be together for two weeks left us weak-kneed. We were booked on a Globus Tour and became known as "the sisters" sometimes just making the bus as it took off for the next stop. We started in Shannon and ended in Dublin. I had a friend, again a nun from USF days, who got us rooms in the Mercy Sisters' Mother House the last night or two and she even got

In front of Mercy Sisters' Mother House in Dublin.

Ed a room the last night way across the quad. I so enjoyed seeing Sr. Mary Hanrahan again - that was just frosting on the cake! After my sisters flew home John and I spent one more week in the garden section of Ireland, beautiful and historical. We learned about WW II and Saint Kevin.

Our last trip for the 1990s was to Africa, November 21 to December 14, 1999. Initially we went to attend the conference of the Parliament of The World Religions. The Parliament was started in 1893 in an effort to bring about peace between people of different religions. Hans Kung's document, "Towards A Global Ethic: An Initial Declaration" written in 1993 and Joel Beversluis's book "A Source Book for the Community of Religions" each chapter written by a member of that faith, were issued to that end. All in all, the organization wants to promote peace among and respect for each other's religion. By this time there were two hundred plus groups calling themselves religions. Interesting!

Hikiing in Africa.

Beyond the Parliament we learned about Nelson Mandela, the diamond industry, the University of South Africa in Cape Town and Cecil Rhodes. The Parliament convenes with people from around the world every five years or so. (Notes from the meeting itself are in the next piece.) We attended this one-week meeting while staying in the college dorms, Smuts Hall at Cape Town University. We had come a week early to go on a safari, see Johannesburg, Robben Island where Nelson Mandela was imprisoned for so many years, as well as the shantytown where he had lived previously. We also stayed two nights at a wine grape farmer's home; he had been an exchange student with our Salinas friend, Todd Kodet. His wife entertained us royally and we learned a lot of history in two days.

The conference speakers were many and varied. The wharf at Cape Town looked as modern as Pier 39 in San Francisco and somehow, we managed to meet our Salinas friend, Joan Moore, the widow of General Jim Moore, for dinner. Her cruise ship had docked for a night ashore. It all seemed magical!

On one Sunday after church, we asked a couple walking out with us where we could get a good dinner that afternoon. They put us in their car and took us to a Kirstenbosch National Botanical Garden with not only a top of the line restaurant but also a superb sculpture display outside in the unlimited gardens. We happily spent the rest of the day there. The menu contained pheasant, grouse, red deer, impala and other items we had never eaten. The whole experience was otherworldly. We took a cab back to the dorms and a life we could recognize.

We spent a few days after the conference taking the train up to Port Elizabeth. Along the way we stopped at the world's highest bungee jump and to take a dip in the Indian Ocean—another thing crossed off my "to do" list. We arrived home via Miami in plenty of time for Christmas with all the little ones.

A Summation of my Impressions of the Parliament of World Religions December 1 - 8, 1999

Visible all over Cape Town were signs both for and against holding this conference here. Before the conference opened we went 1) to the Company's Garden, 2) to view the AIDS Memorial Quilt that took up a whole city block and 3) to visit the Holocaust Museum; a shock—not realizing the Germans and Jews animosity was so visible in Africa during WW II. District Six was the physical staging place for the conference. When entering we received a blessing from three former residents of District 6 as well as a blessing of the five continents and four directions after walking through salt (the tears of South Africa's District 6—all blacks, Jews and Indians). These people were cleared off the land to make it available for white Protestants. The prayer: "May the mystery we call by many names and for whom some have no name bless us here today."

The Parliament of World Religions is about 1) harmony not unity 2) cooperation (convergence) not consensus 3) facilitating projects around the world 4) seeking creative engagement. The week ended with a final blessing by people of many faiths after asking, "Who are you?" First, they blessed the women, then the men then the children accompanied by an American Indian singer from New Mexico, then a Japanese drummer.

The six days were filled with workshops regarding such topics as Spirituality, Global Ethics, Global Aspects of Forgiveness, the World Bank,

Democracies that become non-accountable to the people, and Education — always addressing the question "Does my prayer lead to action?" "How can non-violence, which is passive, lead to positive action in the world?"

We heard fascinating speakers, Ela Gandhi, granddaughter of Mahatma Gandhi — Hindu from South Africa, S. Wesley Ariarajah (Methodist from Sri Lanka), Rev. Hans Kung, Sr. Pat Brombard and Sr. Mary Malady O.S.B. (Order of Saint Benedict), all Roman Catholic, and Dr. Margaret Shanahan, a Jungian Analyst. All addressed such questions as arise through our religion, our spirituality, and our liturgies and how they form us to BE in this world. Are they helping us? How? All agreed religion is needed — not to be combined but to interact peaceably for the greater good. We also heard Bishop Garcia of Chiapas, Mexico speak on Liberation Theology. He told a story which sums up the conference. A priest in Mexico came to a village to say mass. The people said, "Just a minute, we must reconcile first." And they all started to speak to each other — children to parents, men to men, women to women, enemy to enemy and when they were finally reconciled, they told the priest he could continue — sorry for the delay. It took three days! We must learn how not to impose our religion, but how to discover the presence of God in all people.

One workshop was on Mysticism based on Fr. Karl Rahner's writings and quoting Ignatius of Loyola — make choices, discern and seek unity with God and all. Sunday's sermon "If we measure ourselves against the crazies and criminals, we look pretty good. We must measure ourselves against Christ's life and values."

Other speakers — Nelson Mandela, "Religion is necessary when government lets us down. It is our rock and grounding. It educates us and shows us how to accept suffering while working for change in society non-violently."

Rosemary Reuther, "Realize each system has an integrity of its own; true and authentic realities."

There were several talks on race; a judgment based purely on appearance; we are medically all the same, blood types, organs etc. We are each in a body about which people make judgments.

Archbishop Tutu and the Dalai Lama spoke, saying we each have some potential if we drop our bias and seek a deeper awareness. I found the whole week extremely rich and thought provoking. Rick Steves sees travel as a political act. In this case, as in others, I tend to agree with him.

I came away with some new images of religion:

1) Different paths, all going up the same mountain.

2) One mountain, one path (fundamentalism)

3) One big mountain & many hills — other religions only getting you to top of hill.

4) A variety of mountains, all in the same mountain range, all going up. Go to other peaks and look at your mountain.

Statue of Cecil John Rhodes.

RHODES, CECIL JOHN (1853-1902)

I'd heard of him though I'd never thought of him as a great benefactor. Going to the Republic of South Africa last fall brought me face to face with who he was, if not with the man himself. A man of great ambition, he held Great Britain in high esteem, to the extent that he felt the British Empire should rule all of South Africa and to this end he devoted his life.

We first met on a November Sunday morning. John and I were walking into the town of Rondebosch to find a church service and passed a large statue of him sitting in the position of Rodin's "The Thinker." We later found out he had donated the land and the money to build Cape

Town University. We were attending The Parliament of World Religions conference there and staying in the Smuts Hall dormitory. The regular students, and since the lifting of apartheid all can go there, were on Christmas break. It was a brick building covered with ivy, I suppose like our Ivy League universities. Built in 1925, the plumbing and other facilities reflect its age. Our room on the second floor was typical—two twin beds, one desk, lamp, waste basket and closet, one large window, no screen and two book shelves. Appropriate I thought. The shower was downstairs and the toilet down the hall. Having the tank above one's head seemed precarious but there was no doubt the toilet would flush when the chain was pulled. Actually, the toilet was in a room by itself and one first entered a small room with a sink and a mirror. Since it was summer the window was always open and the ivy grew gracefully through it and around the mirror. The couple in the next room rose early and he would be shaving at the sink in plain view when I opened the door to make my first dash to the toilet. His wife (standing in the hall) said, "Oh, go right in. He won't mind." Being in my nightgown, I did mind but there was no help for it.

The dining hall was across the parking lot and since breakfast came with the room ($22.00 a day) we ate there each morning. And what a breakfast it was! We had juices - orange, papaya and guava, then fruit - fresh watermelon, honeydew, cantaloupe, pineapple, mango and papaya as well as the staples of apples, bananas and oranges. A hot breakfast of eggs, breads, two kinds of meat, sometimes pancakes and coffee, tea and milk followed these. Ooh, and I forgot the cereal, either hot or cold and three choices of cold. We were well fortified for the day; as well we needed to be.

When I finally found the laundry room, two flights down and along a deserted hallway in the bowels of the building, my past life as a college student certainly came to mind. We were even so tired we twice had pizza delivered at the end of long days of meetings. Not possible in my day!

We had toured Johannesburg earlier on our trip and seen the diamond mines most of which are the property of De Beers Consolidated Mines formerly owned by Mr. Rhodes. From this rich and powerful position, he set about building a railroad from the Cape to Cairo, parts of which are still operating today though its full length was never completed.

He was as generous as he was ambitious and wealthy. Education was dear to his heart. Born in England and suffering from tuberculosis he went to Africa for his health and to join his brother, a cotton grower. To complete his education he returned to Oxford, England six months of each year from 1873 to 1881. Following his graduation and acquiring the mines he set about accumulating land for the British Empire. He annexed what are now called Botswana, Rhodesia and Zambia and put the British South African Company in charge. He became its chief executive and then the Prime Minister of the Cape Colony. From this position he sought to drive out the Dutch who had settled the cape long before the British came and was very instrumental in defeating the Dutch in the Boer War. However, in a way the war defeated him as he suffered a fatal heart attack before the war was over.

Cecil Rhodes never married and accumulated unprecedented wealth, which he spent freely to enhance the British Empire. It is through his last will that he accomplished the most in bringing England's influence to the rest of the world. He left all his fortune to public service and a huge amount to Oxford University to establish the Rhodes Scholarship Program. Students from all over the world can obtain this two-year scholarship to attend Oxford. During World War II this program was suspended for a time but now has been extended to many more countries than the original few; the British Commonwealth countries, South Africa, West Germany and the United States.

Such generosity should be rewarded and to that end I shall encourage my grandchildren to apply for this scholarship. In our travels around the Republic of South Africa, we found many examples of the Dutch and British influence. It is a country of vast wealth and abject poverty at once primitive and sophisticated. The abolishment of apartheid has brought monumental change to the country and I hope that in time, it will also bring change to the university dorm toilets!

I found this article in our news magazine in August 2015.

Times change and so do attitudes or is it 'Attitudes change and cause times to change'?

SOUTH AFRICA

Tear down this white supremacist

Mzukisi Qobo
Business Day

THE WEEK April 3, 2015

A statue honoring a white supremacist has no place at a South African university, said Mzukisi Qobo. Over the past month, students at the University of Cape Town have begun agitating to get the statue of Cecil Rhodes removed. Several students kicked off the protest by flinging excrement at Rhodes' head, and now the monument stands covered in black plastic while administrators consider its fate. Rhodes is a giant figure in the history of the region. A British mining magnate who bribed his way to become prime minister of the Cape Colony, he was given "unfettered authority to colonize parts of Africa." He sponsored a vile piece of legislation that gave white farmers the right to whip black workers. More than anyone else, Rhodes laid the foundations for apartheid. In later years, he sought to rehabilitate his image through philanthropy, endowing the Rhodes scholarships and giving "vast tracts of his residency" to establish the University of Cape Town. It was "a selfish attempt to atone for his earthly sins," and students and lecturers need not be grateful. Tearing down the statue is just the first step. The historically white university should do more to hire black professors. Instead of statues to whites, we need "black role models."

Newspaper article, South Africa, 2015.

Peach orchard in bloom.

CHAPTER 8—PART 2

MEANWHILE ...

A meaningful event in this decade was a gathering of all my family at the ranch where we grew up to celebrate "Bought the Farm Day." My father had left the ranch to my brother, Vince with the understanding he owned one-seventh of it and had to buy out the other six of us. This day was in May 1992, almost ten years to the day since Mom had died and we were all celebrating though I'm sure Vince and his wife, Betty were the most relieved.

Bought the Farm Day, May 24, 1992.

We wrote a song and videotaped a mock ceremony—all so happy
Vince was succeeding on the ranch and that we were all still friends. We
called the song "Thanks for the Memories" after Bob Hope's song.

Hutcheson Farms label.

THANKS FOR THE MEMORIES

CREATED ON "BOUGHT THE FARM DAY" 5/24/92

THANKS FOR THE MEMORIES--
SWIMMING IN·THE DITCH,
PLAYING "KICK THE CAN"
PLUGGING OF THE RIVERBANK
BY BAGGING SACKS OF SAND.

OH, THANK YOU SO MUCH!

THANKS FOR THE MEMORIES--
STANDING AT THE GRADING TABLE
JUMPING IN THE COTTON TRAILER
PACKING PLUMS, GLEANING NUTS
EATING POMEGRANITES.

OH, THANK YOU SO MUCH!

THANKS FOR THE MEMORIES—
THE HARD WORK THAT YOU'VE DONE
THE FARMING IN THE SUN
THE PARTIES AND THE WALKS
THE LAUGHTER AND THE TALKS

OH, THANK YOU SO MUCH!

About the same time, I became acquainted with a Franciscan priest at the San Juan Bautista Retreat House named Fr. Richard. He was to play a big role in my self-improvement process. He listened patiently and was very encouraging in my efforts to use my degree in spirituality. With his help and that of friends, Bonnie Gartshore who worked for the Herald and Monterey diocese, Merlene Doko, head of the Monterey Diocese School of Ministry and Sr. Patricia Bruno, I organized and put on retreats for several dozen women in '92, '93 and '94. Fr. Richard also introduced me to a new (to me) type of personal retreat called GIM, Guided Imagery with Music. It consisted of a week of solitude speaking only to your guide about the images that occurred while listening to the classical music she chose. As it turned out while meditating on these in silence the images usually connected with some scripture and always had a message. I have attended a week of silence starting in 1992 until this year of Covid 19 and feel it has carried me through many challenges as well as giving me time to reflect with joy on the triumphs in my life.

With all the new people joining our family through marriage and grandchildren, I became interested in the Myers-Briggs personality test and how personalities develop, the grandchildren and mine. I found it fascinating and almost wished I had studied psychology instead of spirituality, though both are of a whole. The purpose of this personality indicator was to make C.G. Jung's theory of personality types understandable and useful in people's lives. It does matter whether you approach the world as an extrovert or an introvert as you gather information differently, process it and make decisions based on aspects of your particular personality. To realize each of these little grandchildren come with a unique set of specifications gave me a lot too think about. Primarily, how do I relate to each of them?

Another personality test popular in the nineties was the Enneagram; sometimes called spirituality by the numbers. The Enneagram divides people into nine basic types, each of which is assigned a number. It is described as "an important tool for improving relationships with family, friends and co-workers." It took me a long time to figure out which number category I fit into, but when I did, it answered a lot of questions about why I behaved as I did and made the choices I had. Somehow this was very satisfying. I can try harder in some areas and let go in others with the knowledge that this is who I am. One of the descriptions of my number is "I remember my childhood as happy" and as I write this, I do!

Fashion Shows

Lo the many! They are used as sales promotions, fundraisers and organizational bonding events. Under sale promotions come wedding dresses, graduation dresses, prom dresses, travel wardrobes, etc.

The first fashion show I remember was as a senior in private boarding school in Hollywood. The graduating class always wore the same white, to the floor gowns and carried one dozen red roses. Weeks, maybe months, before the graduation the senior class was assembled and asked to choose a dress. Several members of the class were chosen to model the dresses from the different stores. The main stores, May Company, Macy's and others each sent representatives to our school with dress samples in hand. Those of us chosen were told in advance that we would meet back stage and be given a dress to model. In this school we'd had lessons in walking gracefully with good posture, neither galloping (as I tended to do) nor slouching hesitantly (as some others did). I donned the dress given me and along with 5 or 6 others walked across the stage several times in front of the rest of the senior class. If I remember right we voted that afternoon. The rest is history! We all looked very nice though I don't think the one I modeled won.

My second experience was as a young housewife when the Junior Chamber of Commerce asked my participation with my husband and our toddler, Catherine, almost 2. We were living in a very small town and were the epitome of the up and coming young families the Chamber wanted

Dee Dee Nucci

MODELING
for
S I M P L Y
Barbara's

at the
C.W.A.
Fashion
Show

Margaret
Marcroft

S I M P L Y *Barbara's*

345 MAIN ST. • SALINAS • 408-757-8611   M C • VISA • AM-EX • SIMPLY BARBARA'S REVOLVING CHARGE

Fashion Show.

to promote as their signature in the community. It was very stressful! I remember coaxing (just short of dragging) my eighteen-month old daughter up the ramp while trying to keep smiling and walking beside my husband on to the stage. There was no more modeling for quite some time, though I dearly loved being active in the Jr. Chamber of Commerce.

Modeling.

Of course, between these two experiences my roommate, Alice and I attended several fashion shows put on by Bridal Shops in San Jose. Being on that side of the lights was also very exciting to this country girl.

Then when the last of the children were away in college and with a little time on my hands, I gave myself a sixtieth birthday present - a real modeling class to learn to apply makeup, more about current hair styles and which colors and styles looked best on me. In the early nineties, having your colors "done" was all the rage. I modeled clothes for Simply Barbara's, the lady's ready to wear shop on Main Street, at Steinbeck House luncheons handing out cards from the store. The highlight of this adventure was modeling for the California Women for Agriculture Luncheon-Fashion Show at the Plaza Hotel on Cannery Row in Monterey. It was their annual fundraiser and great fun! Shortly after as part of my class we had a professional photographer come to take pictures with which to seek further employment. While I was posing, the photographer asked me if I needed the money from modeling. When I replied in the negative, he very seriously advised me not to go into this field. His remarks gave me pause and though I hadn't considered modeling as a career he sounded so protective I suspected he knew something I didn't. I have not been sorry I followed his advice.

Since I'd received my Masters in Spirituality in August '86 I decided to concentrate on that area of interest-a better fit than modeling. In August and December of 1986 Mike and Joan both married. Many weddings followed. In the space of nine years I attended seven weddings as mother of the bride or groom and felt the money the modeling class cost was well spent.

More modeling.

At the Table of Life
A baby's changing table—new since my children
Has become a necessity—so easy on one's back.
Children's play tables with chairs just their size
Give little bodies the control, which they lack.

Removing tonsils, appendix and setting bones
It is the doctor's table that we dread.
The operating table—glaring lights, masked people scare us
Till we remember we have you, Lord sitting at its head.

Table, a place to meet and eat, feast in greatest joy
Where we encourage, implore: mend a broken toy.
Where two or more share sad news—gather to pray
Or take a moment to ask you to bless their new day.

Indoors or out—depends on the weather.
We gather to nourish each other and ourselves.
Later—a place to play games, checkers or cards
All ages welcome as are athletes and bards
We do puzzles, listen to stories and trade jokes
Tales, old and new are told and re-told by some folks.

And the LAUGHTER, oh the laughter that spills from its frame
Rolls onto our laps, down over our feet and on towards the door.
Then with a jolt, we spring up and exclaim,
It was in the blessing—NO—the eating? No, oh no -
It's in the LAUGHTER we really see and call you by name!

LORD!

You are present indeed at our table!

Writing Is

Writing is to remember

>   To clarify

>   To untangle feelings as though emerging from a spider web.

Writing is to record images

>   To stretch vocabulary

>   To see the unseen; filmy images, gauzy likenesses.

Writing is to educate

>   To fabricate

>   To build word towers as in Jenga.

Writing is to link old and new

>   To link past and present

>   To connect words, like colors on a color wheel.

Writing is to link people to people

>   To link people to times and events

>   Most of all, to link you to me, me to you, and us to Passion.

CHAPTER NINE

2000 TO 2010

CAUGHT UP IN LIFE—A WEEK

Sometimes there's just no help for it! We can get so caught up in life, one might say "tangled", that the feeling is one of going down for the third time with little hope of surfacing. That's the way the last week has been.

Wednesday, May 3, 2000: Compile a 'must do' list. Call a neighbor in to see the remodeling just finished two weeks before, as she had been recuperating from surgery so needed to get out for a few minutes. As we visit the front door bursts open and in stumbles John, my husband, who sits abruptly on the step down into the living room, clutching his right arm, sweating and white as a sheet. "I think I dislocated my shoulder", he says. I can see he is in terrible pain. I rush to change clothes and the neighbor flees out the front door. We arrive at the ER just as an ambulance is pulling away. They are very busy. After a half-hour he gets a doctor to come and look. He prescribes pain medicine, and we wait as an ambulance arrives about every 15-20 minutes. After an hour and a half, they take him to x-ray to see if he broke or dislocated his arm. I thought he had been out staining the deck, but it seems he had hiked up the hill behind our house, tripped and tumbled, pitching forward, and landing on his right shoulder.

When he comes out of x-ray, there is another long wait during which I go out and ask the nurse for more pain medicine. She says laughingly, "If he had been shot or had a knife in the chest, we'd get right to you, but a broken bone, you just have to wait. We did call the orthopedist, but he's in surgery." So, we wait. Finally, the doctor comes about 2:30 and confirms it is a break too close to the shoulder to be cast. It will just have to be held in a sling. He prescribes pain pills and sends us home. We drive through a fast food for lunch, call our daughter, Janet, who should be in the hospital delivering to say, "Where are you? We didn't see you at the hospital." Her baby was due May 1st.

John had a very long uncomfortable night, finally dozing off. At 7:00 (AM), the phone rings, daughter Janet is on her way to the hospital. John jumped when the phone rang and was again reminded he broke his arm. Since he is left-handed, it is a blessing it's his right arm.

Thursday, May 4th, Justine Ryan arrives at 1:42 PM, all 10 lbs. 1 oz. of her. I leave John at home, grab a camera and head for the hospital. First, I had to get John new pain pills as the first ones made him sick to his stomach. At the hospital, big sister Rebecca is waiting, yelling, "My baby came out! You want to see her?" Of course! She takes off running and I follow. Her mom's room is the last one down the hall. She knowns exactly which one, so we leave her father walking a sedate pace behind us. Great visit. Get one picture before the battery goes dead on the camera. O.K. Go home to change the airline tickets, cancel John's and set mine to come back a day early from Salt Lake City.

Friday, May 5th, 9:30 AM hair appt. 11:00 AM. It is Grandparent's Day at Sacred Heart, but first, batteries for the camera. Watch a delightful program where our three grandsons, first, second and third grades sing patriotic songs. Since their other grandmother is in Switzerland, I took pictures, drove the boys home and rushed to get lunch for John, and to see if the new pain medicine works. Nope! He is again in danger of losing breakfast… as he had yesterday. Switch to Tylenol, which he knows he can take without nausea. He wants to go visit the new granddaughter. I discover I no longer have my camera. Call grandson's house, not there, call the school, school's closed — half day. I knew that! Eat lunch, take John and go by the school to see if I had dropped it in the field or parking lot. Find a janitor who saw a child turn in a camera to the second grade teacher. I'm reminded of my teaching days — a good janitor is the best that can happen to a school. He describes my camera and says it will be safe until Monday — Monday?! I have to have a camera over the weekend for granddaughter Maureen's first communion in Salt Lake City.

We go on to the hospital. Janet has finished camera's roll of film and wants me to take it to one-hour developing so I can take pictures to her sister, Joan, in SLC. While we wait, John and I pick out two videos to rent for him to watch over the weekend. Go home and call our son to sleep over Saturday and Sunday while I am gone. Start dinner and daughter Carol, from Cupertino, calls to say she is in town to see the new baby. Can she come for dinner and the night? It's an answer to prayer as I leave at 5:45 AM for my plane, and John cannot get dressed by himself. And Carol will also fix breakfast. I still haven't packed and must get instruction on how to use John's camera.

My sister Fran phones, she had just lost her husband and her children have spent the last week getting her through a hospital stay and into a dry-out center. She is crying, saying she is in prison and fears her children will take all her money; they are good people I say, calm her down a bit, finish dinner, Carol comes and we eat.

Another sister, Eileen calls from Seattle and her mother-in-law has just died. Her family is very upset as a distant aunt makes the arrangements, and they are not consulted even though they had taken care of their grandmother for eleven years in Seattle without any help. She was the children's only grandmother. Talk a long time to her... and pack. Give Carol a few instructions, get John ready for bed, and go to bed myself.

All went well with the flight to SLC. Daughter, Joan and granddaughter Maureen met me on arrival. We go to a birthday party to pick up Ross, my grandson, and then home for lunch about 1:00. They have a trampoline in the backyard that is 5 ft. off the ground, and they want me to play. I change my clothes and out we go. I jump about a half dozen times before I realize we don't need two broken bones in our house. I watch them; it is an incredible sight. Their house is on a ridge. The land behind their backyard drops off steeply. Down below, about 200 yards, is a highway and many houses. Across the valley are the snowcapped stiletto sharp Wasatch Mountains. As I stand on the deck and watch Maureen and Ross bounce higher and higher on the trampoline, it seems they are flying in space with this majestic backdrop behind them. I take pictures, hoping they will turn out. We play foosball and build with Lego's. Joan makes dessert for Sunday and Pete mounts some newly arrived padded cornices in the family room. Joan and I get flowers for the table centerpiece and fix dinner. Then it's out to play basketball, watch Ross ride his sister's big bike, and inspect their new camping trailer. I laugh at their mailbox that is a river rock edifice four ft. high and 1 ft. square with a metal mailbox embedded near the top. After a nice but short visit with Joan and husband, it's off to bed for me. At 3:30 AM, I'm awakened by an unrecognizable roar and bang repeated unceasingly. I cannot go back to sleep for a long time. Finally figure out it is the wind roaring and something is loose on the roof above my room that bangs and bangs.

Sister Olivia (on left).

At breakfast, I apologize for laughing about the mailbox - Joan said their old one was constantly being blown down by strong winds. It is pouring rain but by one o'clock, it is dry and Maureen's first communion goes off without a hitch. My 82-yr old aunt, Holy Cross nun, Sr. Oliva joins us and we all have dinner at Joan's. After dinner, we watch the end of a pro-basketball game. Sr. Oliva knows two of the Utah Jazz players personally and Pete is also a big fan. After all the pictures, gifts opening, and food it is time to tell the children goodbye as they will not be up when I leave in the morning. It was a perfect 36 hours with everyone at their best. I hate to say goodbye. Joan arranges for a shuttle to get me to the airport by 6:00 AM. We visit a bit more, then retire.

Sister Olivia at her 90th birthday, 2007.

Pete wakes us up before he leaves. Joan and I have coffee after I dress and pack. The shuttle is on time, I arrive at the airport on time and unconsciously I slip back into my other life. My plane is cancelled. The airlines have made other arrangements for me. Instead of going SLC to SF to MRY, I'll go SLC to Phoenix to MRY with a two-hour layover in Phoenix and won't leave for another hour. No meal is offered on the first leg of the journey. When I get to Phoenix I lie out on a row of seats and go sound to sleep, awaking hungry and afraid I'd overslept. At the gate, I learn I still have another hour and there will be no meal on that flight. I decide to eat, and find I had given the shuttle driver a $50 bill instead of the $20 bill she requested. Wow! Since I almost never have anything but $20s and it was dark in the van, I can see how I made the mistake, but why I did, I don't know. The next flight is uneventful and I arrive home Monday, May 8th two and a half hours later than planned to find John just finishing the last few minutes of the second video we had rented on Friday.

Janet had made it home with the new baby and our daughter-in-law Debbie had filled in with Rebecca for the day. John had had all his meals and needs cared for, the school had called to say that my camera was safe and could be picked up anytime. These intense five days of my life were beginning to untangle, and it's good to come up for air. I find myself gulping great gasps of gratitude for the energy, excitement and equilibrium of them all. But right now, I'd like to take a break before getting caught up in another towering wave of life's events. What a week!

2000 TO 2010

And so, began the new century, not much different from the last, maybe a bit faster pace! Some things stayed constant — tennis for one. Our "C" team won the league both in 2000 and 2001 which caused us to have to move up to the "B" level as that is the rule. If your team takes the title twice in a row, you are too good for that level. Playing at Chamisal after being on the Titus team meant much stiffer competition anyway and Chamisal was to soon begin the September International tournament attended by women from all over the United States and other countries. Though I knew these were "A" players, I entered anyway just for the competition. I usually housed one or two of the women from out of town for fun and we could practice here at The Meadows at off times. Each year one of the supporters donated a towel to each entrant so I have one for each year; 1997 and 2007, local tournaments and 2008 to 2015, international tournaments. Some of the women traveled from hard court to clay court in Houston to grass in Philadelphia. Their husbands accompanied them and they talked of bridge tournaments and dinner parties in the evenings, but there was no convincing John and I wasn't that good anyway.

One of the other things that stayed the same was my involvement in SEEK, the bible study started by Joann Branson. We ladies had a great time having a party or overnight at least once each summer. During the '90s, for 5-6 years, we also attended a weekend religious conference in Los Angeles each February with prominent speakers from around the country. There

On left, Joanne Branson, Founder of S.E.E.K.

were the latest inspirational books as well as religious art items for sale. It was always an uplifting three days.

Speaking of parties, one of the best was a Family reunion held at the ranch in June 2001. Janet designed a T-shirt, an Oak tree of the Hutcheson Family Reunion with the names of us eight Hutcheson siblings on it. With the help of her cousin, Mary Tressel, they ordered one for each person in different colors for each family. Then, my sister-in-law, Betty had a professional photographer come

Hutcheson Family Reunion 2001.

The Marcroft Family.

and take a picture of the whole group. We went swimming in the pool, had mass in the shed and dinner brought in. We all stayed at The Lamp Liter Inn in Visalia and then went back to the ranch for breakfast, tours of the ranch led by my brother, Vince and pictures before all heading home. Sr. Olivia, Dad's baby sister, and his only living sibling, also came from Indiana so all in all it was a huge success.

In July I turned 70 and all the children surprised me with a party at our pool here at the Meadows. A great time was had that evening at our house. Cathy and Joan were in from out of state and we went to Disneyland the next couple of days with them and their kids, Emma, Peter, Maureen and Ross; an exciting adventure to end their stay.

Actually, as the grandkids started grammar school, then high school the next ten to twenty years were spent going to sporting events and graduations. We attended as many as we could, in and out of state. The one very memorable football game was Mason's team vs. Ross's when they were both seniors. One lived in Granite Bay and the other in El Dorado Hills. It was the league championship game. Their mothers bought t-shirts from each school and cut them in half then sewed mixed halves together so John and I each had half a t-shirt for each team. We sat with one daughter's family for the first half and during half time walked to the other side to sit with the other daughter's family. Near the end Mason (defense) tackled Ross (ball carrier) just short of the goal line, ending El Dorado Hill's bid for the championship. Some photographer took a picture and titled it "Just a little hug from a cousin." Mason's team went on to win the state championship in southern California — Mason's last game ever. Ross has gone on to play in the NFL for the San Francisco 49ers!!! But that's another story.

They weren't the only two athletes though. Emma swam for Sarah Lawrence College in New York and her brother Pete went through University of Chicago on a scholarship and played football for them. Mike's boys, Timothy, Paul and Steve played football for Palma High School and some basketball. Jake also played football and his sister, Tess, was in the marching band. Ross went to University of San Diego on scholarship (in spite of being tackled by his cousin). We watched mountain bike and cross-country races with Marina and Collin, girls' basketball, volleyball, water polo and more mountain bike race competition with Rebecca and Justine as well as going to CSU Monterey Bay to watch Katrina play out her water polo scholarship. We drove to San Jose to watch Sydney play soccer. Good thing my minor in college was Physical Education. I at least knew some of the rules and how to keep score for all these sports. It didn't seem that long ago that our children had been so involved in their high school sports. Graduations also came thick and fast, sometimes several a spring. My brother, Vince and I got to meet at Fresno State one June when we each had grandsons graduate in Agriculture at the same time.

During the '80s and '90s I traveled some by myself due to John's business schedule and the fact that my girls were setting up their own homes so no one was home but me. I visited my girls out of town, my sisters out of state and my aunts also out of town.

I also kept reading about Carl Jung's depth psychology and became

Me and Patti Keenan.

connected with the New York Center for Jungian Studies They annually sponsored a conference in Ireland, which I attended twice with a friend I had met at GIM retreats, Patti Keenan. I couldn't get John interested in psychology any more than in tennis. Once he retired, and after some rigorous training, he started volunteering every week at the Monterey Bay Aquarium as a docent. In 2003 Patti and I went to Ireland for the conference, the topic was "Midlife Relationships." Patti and I had only known each other about five years and on the plane over there we discovered her daughter had been a college roommate to my brother, Vince's daughter. Small world. What we did know was we both loved Ireland and psychology so had a great time. Some Jung sayings we learned were:

"The question becomes the journey" and "Life is a very short pause between two mysteries." Somethings to ponder. We also picked up author Virginia Satir's "Credo for Relationships." Interesting reading and worth acting on.

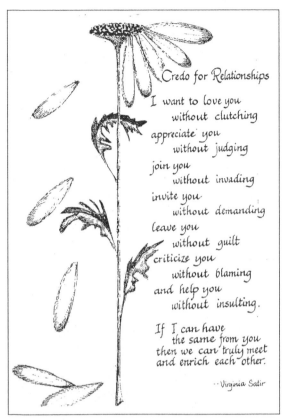

Credo for Relationships.

John and Bettie Bond.

The topic of the second trip was "The Archetype of the Wanderer," which I felt I was fast becoming. This was in 2010 and I was feeling more and more comfortable in Ireland with Patti and this group of professors. They were respectful and accepting of our input though we were not "lettered" in psychology and there were trails to hike and good food. In 2005 I contracted Celiac's Disease so had to eat no gluten. Ireland understood; even McDonalds has "Gluten Free" McMuffins!

Since 2000 John and I had taken several one-week trips through an organization called "Roads Scholar." On one of our first to the Catalina Islands, we met John and Bettie Bond, he a Botany professor and she a Literature professor at Appalachian State in Boone, North Carolina. They had our same wedding anniversary, June 26th, only eleven years later.

They had no children and we had seven but from the beginning we became fast friends culminating in several trips together meeting in Chicago and St. Louis and at the racetracks in Kentucky as well as a visit to each others' homes. The longest trip was a river cruise from Vienna to Amsterdam and then a few days in Belgium in October of 2008. We still keep in contact. My motto, "If I'm in need of a laugh, call Bettie!"

Since we'd had such a blowout for our forty-fifth anniversary, we decided to just have our children's families for our fiftieth in June 2004. We took them for two nights to The Seacliff Inn in Aptos and celebrated Cathy's forty-ninth birthday the first night and our fiftieth anniversary the next night with a disc jockey and private party room. I asked the grandchildren to provide the entertainment not realizing the pressure I put on both them and their parents. All rose to the occasion though with singing, dancing, instrumental music, magicians and standup comics. The youngest, Justine at four, stole the show by involving the whole audience in her recitation of "Ten Little Monkeys Jumping on The Bed." John was having back surgery the next week and Mike had a torn Achilles tendon but none of that mattered that night.

At 50th wedding anniversary.

In June 2005 we participated in the Diocesan Choir trip to Italy. The choir was made up of women and several of our husbands came along. It was a lot of fun and also a lot of work with something like nine performances in ten days traveling from Milan to Rome. Dave and Carol T. stayed over the next week with us at Lake Como, a beautiful place. It was a welcome rest for me as three weeks before the trip I had suffered a ruptured gall bladder. What I didn't know was Carol was suffering from cancer so this was to be her last trip. How she loved to travel!

I had started writing classes and was sporadically sending letters to the editor of our local newspaper and on rare occasions got one published. Current events are important to us all. My goal is to share an outlook of hope and to inspire belief in our democratic government.

Commentary

Bury the past, not the future

By Margaret Marcroft
Guest commentary

Shimon Peres, former president and prime minister of Israel, has passed away. When Thomas Friedman was interviewed about his death, he said, "We let the past bury the past. How can we get the future to bury the past?"

Shimon Peres helped to arm Israel in its early days both by developing weapons and by encouraging the relatively new country to build up its arsenals in its own defense. As he grew older and as time passed, his way of seeking peace indicated, then actually showed him that increasing their military was not a successful way to coexist with other countries.

Once realizing this, he spent the rest of his life seeking "peace" through negotiation, trying to lessen suffering and so was awarded the Nobel Peace Prize. The more mature he became, the more arduous were his efforts. His maturity seems to indicate an answer to Friedman's question. Because the world has engaged in war on some continent at almost any time, we continue to repeat our mistakes and let the past bury our future. With more mature leaders who are willing to live in "real" time with honesty and integrity, maybe we can move toward a future that can bury the past.

All of this is not to say we can ever abolish suffering. It is part of the human condition. As our Congress overrides our president's veto so to allow families who lost members in the horror of 9/11 to sue other countries, I pose these questions. What can be gained with these lawsuits? How will the outcomes aid us in securing our safety in the future? Will restitution to a few (if gained) benefit the many?

Suffering can never be undone or rolled back. No, it can only be transformed into compassion for fellow sufferers, or into a request for mercy for those who do not know what they are doing. Even if justice is gained to some degree, the pangs of suffering will never disappear.

Suffering can also transform us into more mature individuals (if we let it) who can seek to find other ways (than to hit back) to bury our past and strive for a better future!

Margaret Marcroft lives in Salinas.

Letter to the Editor, *Monterey County Herald*, October 16, 2016.

Don't succumb to anger and fear

America has long been the favored son, the country to which many peoples and nations looked for leadership, guidance and deliverance. Now when our security, superiority and comfort are threatened, we act out in fear and anger. Our position has changed from being admired and envied to being seen as debtors and bullies, an adversary rather than an ally.

Now is the time for us to act with maturity and civility as we tackle our problems. No, we the ordinary person on the street did not cause most of the nation's problems but each of us can be a part of solving them. Remaining calm without succumbing to anger and fear will go a long way toward bettering our country and our world.

We have a choice — to act responsibly or not. Let's show the world we can do it without temper tantrums (seen at the town hall meetings) or scare tactics (heard in the fear-mongering rhetoric practiced by some of the media).

Margaret Marcroft
Salinas

Letter to the Editor, *Monterey County Herald*, September 4, 2009.

I also started volunteering at the gift shop at Soledad Mission. Sometimes during Easter and Christmas seasons there are almost too many customers for one clerk, but at other times it was only the field workers who came to visit the chapel. I loved the quiet days, as they reminded me of being on the ranch though no orchards in this valley, only row crops and wind. I have worked there once a month for years until this pandemic shut the Mission grounds down. My friend, Nettie and I would exchange books when she came to tend the roses or help me price items for the shop. She and Jack lived up the road a mile and our children had attended school together. We enjoyed many afternoon visits with our cup of Starbucks she brought from town.

During one of my solo visits to see my sister Dorothy in Ft. Wayne, Indiana we gathered up our aunt, Sr. Olivia—Dad's baby sister who was my babysitter my first two years, and drove to Goodhue and Redwing, Minnesota where Grandpa Hutcheson had started. It was wonderful to see all the places and history we'd heard about as well as to meet the friends, the O'Reillys, who remembered the "Hutchesons who went to California" so long ago. The church where my grandparents were married was still there and the cemetery that held lots of family. The three of us thoroughly enjoyed the trip and I'm so glad we went.

We were back again in 2007 to celebrate Sr. Olivia's ninetieth birthday, then, in May 2008 when she passed away. It was at this time I found out from her friends that she had been a tremendous tennis player in her high school years before her convent days. We had more in common than I thought. She had gone on to become first a nurse, then a hospital administrator for many years as well as one of the Triumvirate to run the Holy Cross order here in the United States for twelve years. It was after that, she retired to live and work in a parish in Salt Lake City where she was a spiritual director. She befriended our daughter, Joan while she lived there, where I visited that fateful weekend in spring of 2000. She will always be missed.

2007 was the busiest year ever, travel-wise. In March we drove to Santa Monica to meet our North Carolina friends, the Bonds. The plan was to spend a day at the park and see the city before we embarked on a Holland America cruise for a two week round trip to Hawaii. But John called us during the night to say Bettie was in the hospital as she fainted getting off the plane. We met him for breakfast and spent the day picking up their luggage, springing Bettie from the hospital and getting medicine so we could embark the next morning. We enjoyed great meals, peaceful waters and topnotch entertainment for two weeks. We stopped at several of the islands but really saw little of Hawaii. The trip itself was uneventful except for learning the game Tri-Ominos. Two weeks at sea was too much for me!

In April the silent meditation group I met with most Thursday evenings started planning a trip to Japan. The leaders, Janet Hoffman and Rev. Hei Takarabi, a retired Presbyterian pastor with the help of a friend, Fr. Thomas Hand, S.J. had secured housing for 14 or 15 of us at a Buddhist monastery and a Shinto shrine. The ten-day trip during cherry blossom blooming was magical, informative and enriching to all one's senses. In Tokyo we attended a Tokyo Giants baseball game-just to ease our transition. We visited gardens, a tea ceremony and many other traditions unfamiliar to us. Shinto is Japan's oldest religious tradition. "Shin" means "the divine being" and "to" or "do" means "way"; not too far from "God's will be done" in the Christian tradition. We meditated at the Buddhist monastery with the monks. Lastly, we took the bullet train to the Hiroshima Peace Memorial Museum. I admit I fully expected to be met with hostility, being American, but instead it was with shear gratitude that they received us. They had grown weary of their leader sending their sons off on conquests

257

and welcomed his end. The most astonishing learning of the trip was about the national attitude; as much as we Americans prize our individuality, they prize their conformity. Because Reverend Hei was drawn to Christianity instead of Buddhism, he had to come to California to practice his faith.

Our last trip in 2007 was in November to the Holy Land in Israel. This trip had been planned twice before but due to political unrest was rescheduled. We started with a tour of New York City where we visited St. Patrick's Cathedral and drove around the devastation of the twin towers; then off to Tel Aviv. This trip was as spiritually nourishing as the one to Japan maybe more so as it was in our own tradition. We started in Nazareth where Jesus spent his childhood and retraced his footsteps all the way to the open tomb from which He rose. We swam in the Sea of Galilee and waded in the Dead Sea. The only hint of the unsettled political environment was in crossing military lines to enter Bethlehem.

The whole year was rich with learning experiences, both restful and charged with energy that expanded our horizons—the real reason for traveling!

One final highlight of the decade was Thanksgiving weekend of 2009 when we gathered all our family from far and wide to join us for a three-day cruise to Ensenada, Mexico. We sailed Friday at 4 pm and arrived back Monday at 8 am. By this time, we had eight granddaughters and eight grandsons so we took up three tables of ten. Each child had a key to their room and though we all disembarked in Ensenada no one lost their key, which was needed to get off and back on the ship. Janet again designed a t-shirt, one for each of us and instructed each adult to take pictures. Little did we know she was planning to compile a picture book for each family for Christmas. People were free to take in whatever activities they chose and were only required to show for dinners and the family picture.

Our own Will won the 'Hairy Chest' contest and many performed at the Karaoke open mic. The ship was the Carnival Paradise; the trip was to commemorate our earlier 55th anniversary. The picture books arrived for Christmas introduced by a poem from Mike and closing with another poem from Cathy. We have relived each moment many times since.

The whole crowd.

Us and grandchildren.

LIFE IS DEFINED BY MYSTERY

Living life is a long journey for most; short for some! Along the way I have found the admonition from my father "to be present and to listen" has stood me in good stead. Too often we think we know the answer when we don't even know the question. Therein lies the mystery. Key questions are: "Why am I here? For what purpose have I come? Why have I survived so long?"

Depending on one's belief system, there are many answers. However, before we've gone very far in life we find that some die young—my cousin Edward, a fourth grader when I was in fifth grade—who fell beneath the truck wheels while jumping on and off the flatbed as his father drove. There was Frankie, an eighth grader hit in the head during a clod fight with a rock embedded in a clod of dirt, the night before our Confirmation. I cried over these deaths but never really thought that might have been me.

As time progressed I settled on what I thought I was to do with my life—teach school. I wanted this with all my being and was bitterly disappointed when I paid $2.50 for an aptitude test where I'd scored highest as a mother, then secondly as a teacher. Later I came to understand my call was to have a large family, to train and educate them in the loving ways I'd learned from my wise and kind parents. For years I saw this as a burden, a repeat of my first 20 years, being the oldest of eight and a hindrance that prevented me from enjoying a responsible position in the community. I now see I was developing a completely new community that has blossomed into a second and third generation. Looking back I can see pluses and minuses, but the key words are "looking back." Not a healthy stance! Standing with one's back to the future usually will cause one to get whacked in the head by what's coming next! The roads not taken will always remain simply issues of idle curiosity.

And so the element of mystery deepens as time passes. The questions persist. What's next? Why am I still here? And what is the purpose for my coming? I'd started out saying, "Yes" to every opportunity and adventure to attain my goals. When in my early forties, I saw most of these goals become unattainable and illusive. Now I began only saying "No." With reflection and re-evaluation I realized I needed to shift my perspective. One day a light dawned. I had been setting my goals, making my plans and because I only sought good things and I worked very hard, I assumed God would approve. Not until my health started to fail, John lost his job, the two older children each wrecked one of our two cars within a week or two did I finally suspect that I may have it backward. Perhaps I should let God make my plans and pray I could carry them out rather than making my plans and asking God to carry them out.

Interestingly, I still remember that insight as though it was yesterday. I'd been saying "Yes" to my love of self and when I adopted love as a way of life—that is, saying "Yes" to someone else, my life has steadily improved. I've learned a lot since then especially about myself. I'm an innovator, an organizer, a gatherer, a communicator and a peacemaker. I know too that Love as a way of life is still a huge challenge. Now that we are entering our "Golden Years" it's clear that what I don't know dwarfs what I do know. And so the mystery continues.

The Star

Rush through the day,
Communicate, pray.
Keep very busy;
Work and then play.
Year after year,

And one starts to wonder,
Even with balance
All's torn asunder.

Then we remember
It's not what we do
It's just being
The one called "you"
That allows others
To be who they are.
This is the wish
God made on the Star.

That star that shone on the world
Over Bethlehem,
Oh so long ago just for you
.... and for me ... and for them.

Time

Thoughts and feelings, within the walls,
above the ceiling of my heart.
Unheralded good deeds pay forward only proceeds
The long road from ambition to fulfillment,
Fraught with detours and missteps.
Could what was hidden from my view
Have inspired me to greater heights? If I but knew.

What have I missed as I raced from past to times ahead?
Never taking side roads, in thoughts and actions moving
straight ahead.
At crossings—impatient with the Red
"What was my hurry?" to myself I said.
A lifetime of Springs, perennially edgy, unending energy
Its bold brightness blinding,
Spring casts an aura of newness on all within view.

Delicious dawn desecrated by daylight saving
Early morning's mellow shades of rose
Time just to be, all rushed away
Cram-jammed into still another noonday.
New babies, new houses, new places and challenges
Delicate dawns fade into such surreal sunsets,
Then kaleidoscope into years I have not yet met.

CHAPTER TEN

2011-2020

In reviewing this last decade, I see I revisit several previous stories but hopefully with a bit more insight. Isn't that what one's later years are for—to reflect? Please bear with me.

This new decade was different in so many ways; lots of losses, celebrations and innovations - CELL PHONES for one, Hybrid cars for another and ZOOM get-togethers.

For the past sixteen to twenty years, we'd been gathering for "cousins' weekends." Us in California, John's sister, Mary, her husband, Chuck in Washington, and their cousins, Jim Weber, his wife Randa in Oregon, and Karla and her husband Ken in Minnesota. It made the most sense to spend three whole days together at alternating residences every other year. These weekends (stopped now for health reasons and Karla's passing) were especially meaningful to me. I did not meet Jim and his sister Karla till the late 1980s, partly because we were all so busy raising our families. When we were married in 1954, only my husband's parents, his sister and brother came, as I said earlier, my religion was a problem for them. It has been a big blessing to now know that getting well acquainted with each other through time spent together and turns hosting at each other's homes

Cousins' Reunion.

has erased those divisions. Getting to know others personally, with time for relaxed discussions can go a long way toward creating harmony in our world. One most memorable cousins' weekend was in Washington, when we all took a day trip to Canada. In this picture we are at Peace Arch Park in British Colombia, how appropriate!

When I was a freshman in high school there was a senior boy who sat behind me in study hall and he owned a convertible. Seniors could go off campus during the noon hour and he frequently drove his convertible around the school block just so we could all admire him I suppose. How I wished for a ride in his car, and though that never happened, I never gave up hope of riding in, maybe even owning a convertible.

Since I was turning eighty in July 2011 John started asking early what I wanted for my birthday. I had always answered his question with the same answer — a convertible! This time I added "and if I don't get one this time, forget it!" Well, he heard me and we went shopping for a convertible, though

Race car driving lesson.

he would not go for a cloth top! We ended up buying a silver Lexus IS 250 convertible with a retractable roof the winter before my 80th birthday. Perhaps the best gift was from the children - a racecar driving lesson sponsored by the Hooked on Driving High Performance Driving Program. I was to show up at Laguna Seca Race Track on a cool November day (11/23/2011) for a lesson in race car

Children singing.

driving. There was a group of us, and I definitely was the oldest. First, we filed into a classroom to study a map of the track and a lesson on what the different colored flags meant—a lot to learn. Next,

Chuck and Mary.

the instructor drove my car to show me the course, and then back to the classroom for more instruction. Next, I got to drive with an instructor in the car and then lunch. At lunch several asked me if I was the 80-year-old. After lunch I got a new instructor who said it was a good sign that my passenger seat was dry!?! Janet and Jim showed up and made a video of me driving as fast as I could, complete with helmet. It really was a thrilling experience and I feel it also made me a better (if faster) driver.

In the July before the lesson, we celebrated my birthday here at The Meadows clubhouse with current and old friends. The children composed a song for me as they usually did at our anniversary gatherings. This time grandson, Steve accompanied them on his guitar. My eighth-grade girl friends, Margaret and Shirley came as well as current friends and tennis

My siblings and spouses Elizabeth, Vince, me, Pat, Candice, Betty and John.

people. We were also privileged to entertain Irene and Clyde. Irene has fixed my hair since I moved to Salinas in '64 — still does — and Clyde took the videos of most of the children's weddings. They're like part of our family. It was a good mix of friends. Janet had a huge poster made of me in my convertible for all to sign. There were friends from the Mission Soledad, Jack and Netti as well as people from the book club, Marilyn and Bob, Merci and Larry. Yes, Marilyn, Merci, Marybeth and Margaret had started a book club around 2005. It is still going, though not all members' names start with "M."

In August 2011 we drove my convertible to Washington, as my sister, Eileen, hosted a Hutcheson reunion there and I got to take my sisters for a ride. On the same trip we also visited John's sister and her husband in Bellingham and my college roommate, Alice, in Yakima. We had some fun times with the car but after three years John felt we should trade it in for a hybrid and that was a good move, the new car has lots of safety features for us "old folks."

My sisters and me.

We drove the new car to Salt Lake City where my husband's brother, David, lived and not being very well, hadn't attended cousin weekends. In the spring of 2012 David died and when we returned from his funeral so had our beloved Sue (of Sue and Bob), who had stuck by us through thick and thin and with whom we liked to vacation. Her passing was very unexpected and seemed to open the door to more losses of friends, two sisters, Frances and Dorothy, and Fran's daughter, Mary before this decade ends.

Dorothy's 75th Birthday dinner.

When Dorothy found she had lung cancer, Eileen, Elizabeth and I went to visit her in Indiana and celebrate her 75th birthday, November 14, 2016. Eileen brought her scrapbook of our trip to Ireland and we reminisced for hours, then went out to dinner thoroughly enjoyed each other's

Human pyramid at birthday celebration.

company. Our brothers, Vince and Patrick made their own trips to say good-by and Patrick (at Dorothy's request) stayed to the very end.

Another ritual that began in 2005 for which I am only a spectator is a special type of birthday gathering. When Janet turned 40 in the same calendar year Cathy turned 50 Janet decided it would be fun for just the seven of them to spend a weekend together sans spouses and children. They booked two double rooms at the MGM Grand—one room for the early risers and one for those who didn't. I got the idea to buy each a t-shirt, which read: "Mom loves ME the Best." They got a lot of notice, they said, walking around the MGM Grand! Their latest venture was to Truckee in spring of 2019 when Terri and Joan were both 60 for a month. Our children don't always agree, espe-

Children in Truckee, spring 2019.

cially on politics, but we're grateful all agree family relationships are of the utmost importance.

During this decade great strides were made by the grandchildren — four made the big leap! Jake and Mary, Marina and Dereck, Paul and Sydney and Tess and John who tied the knot on Zoom September 23, 2020 (another reason to love the new technology). We now have two great grandchildren, Ryland and Brynnley. Because of distance and Covid-19, we don't see them much, so I really appreciate CELL PHONES for the camera, and the ability to text. I can send texts to grandchildren (all grown-up) just to say "Hi", and they can answer or not and sometimes days later and no one is offended.

Ryland Warwick age 4½.

Brynnley Roelle,
age 1½.

In March of 2013, the four of us who had boarded at Immaculate Heart spent a weekend in Cambria and visited Hearst Castle. Between the four of us we had 23 children, all good kids. It was fun to share stories and give thanks for old times, our good health and how far we'd come since our good old days at boarding school and Balboa Beach. It was a great last hurrah! Margaret and I attended two more reunions in May 2014, when I drove my GPS friendly car to Hollywood, and in 2019 when Margaret's daughter, Sally drove us. She enjoyed seeing the sights and the location of our many adventures in the 1940s.

The good ol' days at Balboa Beach.

March 15, 2013

Immaculate Heart boarders, 2013 in Hearst Castle. Me, Margaret,
Eleanor, Katie and Connie.

In June 2014, John and I celebrated our sixtieth wedding anniversary at the The Meadows clubhouse and almost all were able to come. We played games and Jan's friend, Richard Green, took pictures of the group and of each family with G'ma and G'pa. It was fun to see the update from our 2009 trip on the good ship, Paradise. All the grandchildren had grown so much.

60th Wedding Anniversary party.

My 85th birthday in July 2016 was also memorable. John gave me a gift certificate for a Spa Day at Bernardus, but that's no fun alone, so I asked my six daughters to accompany me. After relaxing massages, we enjoyed a wonderful lunch and a relaxing afternoon in the pool. We returned to the house to a bar-b-que dinner fixed by the guys. An all-around special day!

In September 2017 the Women's Tennis Association (WTA) moved the fall tennis tournament south to La Quinta from Chamisal and since I

My 85th birthday.

had entered a new age bracket with my July birthday, I wanted one last shot at a gold tennis ball though my granddaughter, Justine, told me I could always order one from Amazon if I didn't win. In the 75 and over bracket my partner and I did get a certificate from WTA ranking us nationally - but no gold or even bronze tennis ball jewelry. I found a partner and though we didn't win, it was fun to say we played at noon in 95-degree weather in the 85 and over group. My prior partner, Julie, who now lived in Orange, California met my plane and generally hosted me for a week. My son, Mike and his wife, Debbie came down to watch. It was a fun trip, and I did get a shirt out of it. My thanks to all who made it possible.

Playing tennis.

CERTIFICATE OF USTA NATIONAL RANKING

THIS WRITING CERTIFIES THAT

Margaret A Marcroft & Yvonne Merrick

HAS EARNED A NATIONAL RANKING IN THE UNITED STATES TENNIS ASSOCIATION
FOR THE YEAR 2014 AS FOLLOWS:

Women's 75 Team Doubles
DIVISION

22
USTA NATIONAL RANKING

APPROVED BY THE RANKING REVIEW BOARD,

CHAIRMAN OF THE BOARD AND PRESIDENT, USTA

CHAIRMAN, ADULT/SENIOR COMPETITION

Certificate of USTA National Ranking.

277

Me and Julie.

Us with Elizabeth and Joe.

Our last big trip was June 30th to July 14th when we traveled with my youngest sister, Elizabeth and her husband Joe, to Alaska via Holland America. The first three days were on board ship from Vancouver, British Columbia to Skagway, Alaska where we continued on land by every means of transportation possible except horse. I am the oldest in my family and Elizabeth is the youngest so in addition to her living in Arizona, us in California we are fifteen years apart so never spent as much time together as we would like. We have similar interests in family and spirituality. Each of us, in our own communities, has started a spirituality group in which women our age could freely discuss our faith journeys and, we find the same things funny. You might say we laughed our way across Alaska! Joe and John just shook their heads.

It truly was good to have had such a fun trip as soon after, in December, John started his surgery marathon - two new knees, a hernia repair, and one new shoulder. Needless to say, things have slowed down a bit. John did get to his 22nd "Real Birthday" in 2020 when he turned 88. As many grandkids as we could gather surprised him here at The Meadows clubhouse.

Throughout this decade's distractions and obstacles, I have faithfully continued my writing classes with Ilia Thompson at the Carmel Community Center until this virus.

DEAD POETS SOCIETY

These last few weeks, nay months have been a round of parties given by family in every case; starting in April with a baby shower and ending this past Friday with a special graduation. The parties included a wedding anniversary gathering, a family reunion, four birthday parties, a bon voyage party, and a party for the culmination of a dream.

The baby shower was for Mary, the mother of our first great-grandson who arrived conveniently on our sixty-second anniversary, June 26, 2016. The occasion was marked with celebration phone calls, texts, pictures and emails congratulating all on ushering in the first of a new generation. This special birthday fell on the day after our family reunion and many were still gathered. Since the last family reunion was sixteen years ago, we needed this one as the grandchildren just kept growing. The band that played for our son's wedding thirty years prior came out of retirement for us, brought their wives and generally enjoyed themselves as much as the guests.

Between that birth on June 26th and the 13th of August 2016 three birthdays were duly noted with much merrymaking and rejoicing. Then hostess with the mostess, our eighteen-year-old granddaughter, Rebecca, invited all who had influenced and loved her to that point so she could tell them thank you and good-by as she was leaving for a gap year in Spain.

Her mother, Janet, suggested she invite only those who were special in her life and was blown away when she invited one hundred twenty-five people — ages ninety-one to seventeen and her six-week-old nephew. Janet rose to the occasion and it was quite a gathering!

John and I spent the next two weeks at the cabin to stay out of the forest fire smoke and to entertain friends. Then in August daughter, Carol, called us together to celebrate her son, Collin's attainment of his AA degree. It had been quite a journey. He is a mountain biker who broke a couple of bones during the three-year process, as well as winning first place in his age group at the Laguna Seca Sea Otter Classic competition. He was employed at a professional bike shop where he built bikes from scratch and can resolve any bike issue you might have. He now works at Stanford Linear Accelerator Center.

On September 4th we traveled to Exeter, a small valley town near the ranch where I grew up and is still farmed by my brother's sons, to celebrate my sister-in-law, Betty's eightieth birthday. Since she is the youngest of eight and I am the oldest of eight, all who could make it were invited and CAME! My children and grandchildren did not come but hers did and she has just as big a crowd. She included all her siblings and all of mine.

Joan's nursing school graduation.

But the party to end all parties this year was in Reno. Joan, our middle daughter, who has always wanted to be a nurse, finished a two-year course and received her RN on a Friday afternoon. Her 25-year-old daughter, Maureen "pinned" her and there were tears all around. She has quite a support group in Reno as she lived there previously when married. This group of women, their husbands and friends from her past life, as well as four of her siblings and parents came together to celebrate her accomplishment. After being a stay-at-home mom for twenty-five years, she now is successfully launched into her second career. It was indeed the best party of the year!!!

Today while resting up from our mad happy weekend, our granddaughter, Rebecca, texted, asking us to return her CD, the movie *Dead Poets Society*. She wanted to see it once more before leaving for Spain on Tuesday. Since we had not yet viewed it, we immediately sat and watched it. I can almost feel the sentiment taught by that movie running through the generations of our family, "Be who you are, rather than conform to someone's idea of who you should be and seize the moment—Carpe Diem!" How fitting that we should be reminded at the end of a long summer of practicing just that.

Rebecca Warwick.

Exhaustion by Technology

On Saturday the 5th my husband wanted to go to the show. I agreed to accompany him after reminding him of the other things on my plate that day. We decided on the 1:40 showing so we would not miss the sports events later that day.

After returning home about 4:30 pm, I said I would record the U.S. Open on our DVR since he wanted to watch the Giants' baseball game on at the same time. Earlier our daughter had texted the link with which we could live-stream her son's football game from University of San Diego at six pm. I thought through what I would prepare for dinner and then asked for the link listed on his cell phone. He could not find it. I went into my computer to try to find it, asking him to text our daughter and get the link back. Then the land line phone rang, and it was his cousin in Minnesota. Since she seldom calls, I suspected the worst but no, she just wanted to visit. After a while as time was running out, I asked her if she wanted to talk to John, and she did. I took the phone outside and gave it to him, trading it for his cell phone since in the meantime he had secured the link from our daughter for the football game. In my office I managed to make the link work on my laptop so unplugged it and took it to the family room where the Giants' game was in progress and I could start to prepare dinner.

John's off the landline and dinner is ready. We sit down with the laptop on the table in front of the TV to eat. Within minutes my cell announces a text message, "Mom, did you see Ross catch that pass?" Feeling proud as a peacock as we had seen the catch, I told her "of course, good job." By the third quarter the laptop went dead and needed to be recharged. I carried it back to the office and plugged it in. John cleaned up the kitchen having lost interest in the Giants as they were losing. We watched some more of the live streamed football game from San Diego, but they were also losing; we switched to the recorded tennis. For a short bit we watched tennis before totally collapsing from an overdose of media.

Just because I can doesn't mean I should! But as a person whose home didn't even have a phone until I was sixteen, I marvel at the leap.

A Family Gathering

Birthday parties are unpredictable at best — whether for 100-year-olds or for two-year-olds. At this weekend's party, in June of 2018, we celebrated Ryland, our great grandson turning two.

The gathering was in Clovis where, to begin with, the temperature is one and a half times ours here in Salinas on most summer days. All were gathered in the backyard where mister fans ran continually, stationed on either side of the outdoor patio and pointed toward the center. The patio faces the huge backyard where there was a kiddy pool, full of water and plastic animals as large as the two-year old, a slide and swings set all made of brightly colored plastic. When we arrived, we joined Ryland, his mom, three grandmothers, two granddads, one step-granddad, several aunts and uncles, plus one great grandmother; I made the second. One grandmother and one aunt are Chinese and had married into the family several years back. When they joined the family they had not ever met before and were from different parts of China but over the span of several years had become the best of friends. They respectfully and lovingly tended their husbands' (who were brothers) mother, the other great grandmother, and immediately showed me the same care and attention. They laughed at their efforts in speaking English.

Two other families, day care friends of Ryland, came next, one with one child the other with two and a third to be delivered any moment. This mom voiced concern over having three children under four sometime in the next week or two and I told her I was living proof it could be done. Then I told her about mine checking in as a towhead, the next with fire red hair and the third as a dark brunette. People I met were so intrigued with the hair color they forgot to comment on the ages of my children.

Soon Ryland's dad, Jake appeared, and the meal was quickly laid out on the tables next to the house on the patio. It was a taco party complete with enchiladas, tacos, beef, chicken, beans, guacamole, mango salsa,

Ryland's party invitation.

hot salsa, veggies, fruit bites and no end of chips, soft drinks, water and beer. All this before ice cream and cake! It didn't matter that no one was of Mexican decent. Shortly, Ryland with the help of his mom and dad blew out the large number "2" candle on the cake and dessert was served.

Ryland was quite shy with the guests his age and spent most of his time with his dad and two grandfathers as well as his Aunt Justine. After the dessert, it was time to open gifts; dump trucks large and small were highly favored, nothing else really mattered. As the children left with their parents, Ryland seemed to loosen up and start to really enjoy himself. Some formal pictures were taken of the adults, all the men, then all the women with the Chinese ladies making sure we two great grandmothers had chairs front and center while all others stood around us. Most of these people I had met once before though one of the grandmothers brought a German man few had met, another heavy accent but no problem.

As the sun set, a cool breeze kicked up and the moon came out. All remaining guests helped store left over food, clear the decorations, fold up extra tables and chairs and in minutes all was back in order. In the meantime, Grandpa Jim bathed Ryland and had him ready for bed.

I don't know why I'm recording this except when I think of the age span - preschoolers, teenagers, 30 somethings, 55-65s and three 80 plus, then throw in the ethnic backgrounds, various marital relations and food preferences and the 105-degree weather it seems a lot could have gone wrong, but there was not a single hint of discord or mayhem. Not a tear shed! I'd say our politicians could learn a lot from this gathering!

Well done, Mary!

Ryland Warwick,
age 4—Happy boy.

My Day at Levi Stadium—11-11-18

For each home game of the San Francisco 49ers my daughter, Joan has been getting two free tickets as her son plays on the team. She has been taking different sisters as her guest but today was my turn. We met at Terri's house in San Jose and called an Uber to take us to the 49ers' stadium (new to me though I am an original 49er having graduated from high school that year). The driver was pleasant and knowledgeable about the entrances to the stadium. Before leaving her place, Terri presented us with two salmon spinach salads (to satisfy my allergy to gluten) in clear plastic containers. We packed credit cards, I.D. and other essentials in a clear plastic carry all, per stadium rules. After asking Terri to watch where Dad put his glasses and credit card (they were going to a sports bar for dinner and to watch the game) we sped away. Nearing the stadium my daughter, Joan felt we should get out, but the driver assured us he could get us closer. Finally, with the walking ramp in sight Joan said we're getting out here. We each opened our doors and fled to the sidewalk as a policeman shouts, "you can't let them out here" and our driver yells, "she is an old woman, she needs to get closer." I'm running across the street.

After walking a few blocks, we present our tickets to security who promptly requests our salads. I ask what they will do with them and the girl turns to her supervisor. Joan says, "she looked online and it says anything in clear plastic is admissible." Much discussion: we get in WITH salads.

Entering the stadium, we meet up with the rest of the party to get

Ross and me.

passes to the infield area. We are right below the box suites at about the 50-yard line. Joan had been notified that Ross would be able to see visitors between 3:30 and 4:15, before the game. His father and his wife, Ross' girl friend, Danielle, Joan and I all troop down the stairs (carrying the spinach/salmon salads). Many hugs and pictures! As we visited with No. 82, tight end, Ross Dwelley, a woman touched his arm and asked if he would be offended to have a picture taken with her son; he was a man with Down's syndrome in a wheelchair. Ross jumped at the idea, hoisted the man to a standing position, gave the mother's camera to his girlfriend and asked the mother to join the picture. Danielle took several then handed the camera back to the woman. All were beaming! Including me! As visiting time ended, we trooped back up to the lounge to devour our salads with a beverage. We shared a table with people from El Dorado Hills where Ross had attended middle and high school. Eating together seems to bring out instant new friends.

As we prepared to walk to the end zone to our seats, Joan's ex, who always buys seats on the 50-yard line four rows up, says the first three rows in front of them are unassigned, why not sit there till someone claims the seats. We do!

As the game begins, vendors appear at intervals offering boxes of licorice, M & M's, popcorn and water. All is free to Joan and me but the people behind us have to pay. We quickly realize we are in the "high rollers'" seats available to people up in the suites who might want to stretch their legs and sit outside awhile. Gradually a group of men appear but there is still room for us. As conversation develops one fellow asks my daughter if she works for Mark. With a straight face, she replies, "Mark works for me." He soon disappears and we have the seats for the rest of the game.

Joan, me, Ross and Danielle.

The game itself was very exciting especially the first half when the 49ers were ahead. Ross played only on special teams this game so spent most of his time along the sidelines encouraging other players as they entered and exited the game or turning to urge the crowd to cheer. He is a special grandson.

All gather after the game, a bit frustrated at the loss. We are transported, by Ross's dad, to dinner at Lalla's Grill and I marvel at the congeniality — Ross and his dad in front seats, Danielle, me, Joan, ex's new wife, Liz, in the backseat. Ross's high school friend, who works nearby and had been at the game, joins us. Ross calls Uber again and Joan and I are transported back to Terri's house.

We find my husband has gone to bed and Terri is near tears as she tells me they could not find his glasses at evening's end. She is 99% sure he brought them home from the sports bar. She called, and they didn't find them. I feel that they must be in the house so let's just go to bed. We'll look for them tomorrow. In bed my husband is still awake and says, "I can't find my glasses." Let's sleep on it. The next morning as we four are about to gather for breakfast, I look around our bedroom and bathroom for the missing glasses. As a last resort I open my husband's zipped toilet kit and there are the glasses. I put them on and go to the breakfast table. All exclaim, "Where did you get those?" Happy ending to a great adventure!

Fran and me.

REMEMBERING FRAN
Frances Louise Hutcheson Sangiacomo
December 3, 1935—February 20, 2015

My first vivid memory of Fran and me together is of riding our horse bareback, without permission, and falling off. I broke my arm, and she was bruised. I was just about a week from turning nine and so she must have been almost five. Mostly during grammar school years, I remember arguing over who was the oldest. Fran shot into puberty passing me in height and energy in her seventh grade—my tenth. She consistently told people she was the oldest. The summer I was fourteen I got a job babysitting my cousins at their house in town. Aunt Peggy and Uncle George worked day and night at their Mom-and-Pop grocery/diner across the street from the cannery. I was on call for the children six days and nights a week so that left Fran at the ranch with most of the housekeeping chores alongside Mother. At sixteen I transferred to a boarding school in Hollywood for my junior and senior years, this left Fran with more chores and, since she pictured herself born under a "Big City Star", she was not happy with me. When I came home to attend the local junior college, I remember fighting over clothes, as by then we were about the same size. The other memory of that time was in the summer of '51 between the end of junior college and enrolling in San Jose State, I was in an automobile accident on the ridge route with my girlfriend and went through the windshield causing me to need stitches. Since Mary Lou's car was totaled, I had to call Dad to come get us. We were

at a hospital in Northridge about four hours from the ranch and it was dinner time. I was worried about Dad driving so far since he'd been up since five am. He said he'd bring Fran with him because she would talk all the way and keep him awake. Dad drove from seven pm till five am and she did a good job keeping him awake.

The next memory of Fran is only of our clashing schedules; I graduated San

On Fran's Wedding Day.

Jose State the same day she graduated Visalia High School, Mom went to her graduation and Dad came to mine. After that Fran got her wish to come to the big city and enrolled in St. Mary's School of Nursing, while I taught school in Campbell, California. The four and a half years difference in our ages meant we just kept missing each other, as far as spending much time together. We both soon married and managed to be maid and matron of honor for each other. We lived in different cities while having our families though we tried to get the cousins together as often as possible. Mostly they (we) spent time together at the ranch during the summer. Here we could also spend time with our brother, Vince, and his family.

Time does have a way of marching on and I was always going to do more things with Fran, spend more time with her as we had such fun when we were together. With the death of her first husband Joe in 1971 and a month later the death of our brother Bill, her life took on a surreal quality as she set about raising four children by herself in San Francisco. She found herself in the office of a psychologist rather depressed. After hearing her story, he asked her to close her eyes and imagine one large barrel on either side, telling her to put all her troubles in the barrels. After a short time, she looked at him and said, "Do you have any more barrels?"

This story about Fran helped me through some of my own hard times. Through circumstances and her own doing, Fran's life was not easy, but she had a heart of gold and was extremely generous. She loved the city life and was the life of any party. The saddest day of her existence was when she had to quit working, as her profession had become her identity. I would like to have had the presence of mind to say at her Celebration of Life that even though spending more time and having more laughs together was not to be, we certainly admired each other from afar. Fran's son, Patrick orchestrated a gathering of which she could be very proud. She has been laid to rest beside her faithful George on the gorgeous San Francisco Presidio grounds with three of her four children (Mary was too ill to attend) and five of her six grandchildren present. Her sons Patrick and Michael and daughter Beth all spoke at her send off. She never lost her indomitable spirit through all the adversity she endured. I remind her children and grandchildren that her legacy is this strength of spirit which is available to them if they just ask for it. Farewell, Fran.

70TH REUNION MEMORIES, CLASS OF '49—MAY 5, 2019

Attending my high school reunion with my friend from childhood, Margaret Fitzgerald Burroughs, brought back so many memories of both my friendship with Margaret and my faith journey through the years.

Margaret and my parents were friends in the small rural community of Visalia and both families attended St. Mary's Catholic Church. From the time we were about five or six years old, we have many memories of time spent together both playing at each other's home as well as of the major stages of our lives. This past weekend I was reminded of making our first Communion and Confirmation together, as well as graduating from the same grammar school and high school and then marrying on the same day in St. Mary's. We each married a "John" and even used the same flowers for the church from the only florist in town with our parents sharing the bill. We both taught school that first year out of college, then married and had our first child within a couple months of each other, as well as our second within a year and a half of our first. From then on, we stayed too busy to visit or even see much of each other until twenty years ago when we started going to reunions together and really visiting again.

But the story I want to tell is my faith story! A catechist, who came to our house after school, prepared me for my first Communion. Margaret attended the Catholic School in town, so learned her catechism there. Our two groups were combined, however when the day came, neither of us could attend the class first Communion, as we both had the measles. Two weeks later the kind Sister at St Mary's Catholic School had all the other children come back again all dressed in their white dresses and veils, white shirts and black pants, so Margaret and I could make our first Communion with our class and this time a photographer came and took the class picture. How Sister managed this without e-mail, I don't know.

Confirmation was traumatic as well. During the night before that occasion one classmate, a favorite boy, died in an accident. It was announced at mass in the morning and I found it hard to prepare to meet the Bishop that afternoon. And then he picked me to question. At this point my family had transferred to the Catholic school in town. Sister had warned us the Bishop might question someone in the class. He asked which way of saying the Our Father would give us the most grace: 1) rattling it off quickly and perfectly or 2) saying it while being constantly interrupted or distracted and having to struggle to complete it? I said struggling to complete it would get you more grace. He called me "his little theologian" as I filed past him on the way out of church.

Then came graduation; Margaret and I graduated eighth grade with two other girls and nine boys. She immediately began high school at Immaculate Heart in Hollywood while I went by bus from the farm to Visalia High. At the end of my sophomore year my father offered me a choice. Things were going well and if I wanted, I could transfer to Immaculate Heart and board for the last two years of high school. If I did that, I would have to come home for two years of junior college before transferring to finish at San Jose State or I could stay at Visalia High and spend four years at San Jose State. I had planned to get my teacher's credential there since 4th grade when Sr. Paula was so influential in my life. I chose to go to Immaculate Heart with Margaret that fall of 1947. The next two years were filled with adventures never to be forgotten. Between the first day of school that fall, and Thanksgiving I experienced a bout of homesickness also never to be forgotten!

My dorm was situated on the second floor to the west of the chapel and entry parlor. Junior year I slept in the dorm with seven other girls, then as a senior I had a bedroom with just one roommate, Claire Tona, a junior. My parents and Margaret's took turns delivering us to and from school. I remember it as a long four hour or more trip, which our parents always made round trip in one day. When they were unavailable, we rode the Greyhound bus with the other Valley Girls; Phyllis and Peggy Nunes from Hanford and two from Delano, Mary Ann Zaninovich and Ann Tudor. If we were lucky, we would get the "singing bus driver." We were in the school choir and loved to sing. This driver knew all the latest songs. There were always quite a few servicemen on the bus; they joined in and the four hours sped by.

Because the chapel was so close one could literally slip out of bed, trip down the stairs and be at mass in 20 minutes or so. It was so easy I took to doing it daily. Soon the priest asked me to assist by intoning the Latin responses while kneeling at the altar railing. I could not cross over or touch the cruets, paten or chalice, but I was to ring the bells at the consecration. I seem to remember saying the Our Father in Latin also, since this was before Vatican II, the congregation said nothing. Perhaps I was one of the very first girl altar servers! I was there most days those two years and felt very privileged. No wonder the nuns thought I had a vocation to the convent! Years later I looked on that time as a period of depositing grace in my account freely and easily; grace was in abundance. Ten years later, overwhelmed by challenges, I imagined myself making daily withdrawals. Now, seventy years later, I still feel there is plenty of grace in my account.

After our seven children were fairly independent, on their own, in college or finishing high school, I enrolled in a four-summer course at USF which included one summer on the thirty-day Ignatian Retreat and the other three in classes; all geared toward a MAS degree—Masters in Applied Spirituality. This started as an effort to prepare myself to lead scripture study classes at night during the school year for a friend, Joann Branson, who had written a study program as part of her Doctorate in Divinity. It turned out to be helpful in many other ways. I graduated in 1986 and immediately following in August our son got married, and in December the first of our six daughters married. From then on it was a couple of decades of weddings, babies, graduations and travel, all the while continuing annual eight-day retreats and working for the church.

My first job at Sacred Heart while going to USF was to interview couples preparing to baptize their infants and talk about their faith journey. Shortly after I graduated, we changed parishes, after twenty-five years at Sacred Heart, we joined St. Joseph's in Spreckels and moved to a house in that parish where we still reside. At this parish I was asked to attend formation to learn how to establish the RCIA at St. Joseph's, which I then led for several years. At the same time, I co-taught with Fr. Mike Miller for the School of Ministry then operating in our diocese. As our diocese began to acquire property in Monterey and to expand the diocesan offices, the School of Ministry could no longer be funded and was closed.

In the midst of running RCIA for my parish and organizing weddings for our other five daughters, I served on a committee of eight women from all over our diocese reviewing and making suggestions to Bishop Joseph L. Imesch for his proposed pastoral letter on women, called "Partners In the Mystery of Redemption." I still have copies of the report we sent and am still in touch with those committee members still living. The letter sought to clarify the role of women in the church and be a teaching in inclusivity. It never got past the first draft and its responses. We submitted the letter to committee in August 1988. No further attempts to clarify women's roles in response to Vatican II documents seems to ever have been officially launched.

Our bishop at the time, Bishop Shubsta, asked me to partner with Fr. Larry Kambitsch in canvassing the parishes to establish the willingness of pastors to create a Diocesan Pastoral Council. For three years we traveled and met with every one of the forty-five pastors in our diocese, organized meetings and training of laity to form a Pastoral Council. We found more were willing to sign on than not, though enthusiasm was not universal. Bishop Shubsta died in late 1991 just as our council had finished forming. He had been our bishop since January 1982 when Bishop Clinch retired. His successor, Bishop Sylvester Ryan did not continue with the Diocesan Pastoral council.

For the next several years, my husband and I traveled quite a bit as he'd sold his business in 1994. As family responsibilities again decreased and our enjoyment of travel lessened, I again became active at St. Joseph's as a lector and Eucharistic minister. At some point in the early 2000s our single priest (for a parish of approximately 800 families) took it upon himself to train eight of us who regularly were lectors as "Lay Presiders." We were given a binder that included the "Order for the Celebration of the Liturgy of the Word with Communion." We were to conduct a service, on appointed days, and include a prepared reflection on the readings of the day. A Eucharistic minister from the congregation would distribute Communion. Though it took a bit of time to adjust the members of the parish were given a Communion service and daily spiritual sustenance in addition to the days Fr. said mass. People came to appreciate these services. At first, I grumbled at the work involved, but soon came to know and love preaching as my passion. So much so that on Mother's Day, 2016 our Pastor asked me to deliver a reflection to the parishioners at the nine o'clock mass, that reflection follows. Shortly thereafter our parish was assigned an assistant priest and now "Lay Presiding" has just gone away.?.

Since grammar school, I've sung in a church choir as well as an adult choir for the ten years from 2000 to 2010. My voice seemed to fade after 2010 and now in 2019 I find I can no longer lector as I am constantly clearing my throat. For the past six years, during the school calendar year, I have conducted a spirituality group. We discuss a book of interest to the group that challenges our faith understanding. The gatherings also form community here in the parish. One need not be Catholic or female to come.

My faith story as I call it, is only one side of my life; we are each a multi-faceted creature. I try to seek growth equally, physically, mentally and spiritually. Granted it leaves me a bit fractured, but I like writing letters to the editor one day, my memoirs the next, playing tennis or exercising every other day. Book club and constant contact with my nuclear family as well as my children and their children are more than enough to stretch me and remind me of my sacred relationship with God.

I do find it imperative to remind myself of the separation between God and Church. Here in June 2019, I understand that our diocese may have again formed a Diocesan Pastoral Council, a new School of Ministry and has disbanded the Board of Spirituality. It has organized a School of the Diaconate which is very successful in producing deacons as well as a few new priests. And so, the organization of Church as an entity goes on but the laity remains somewhat removed, made to feel less than it seems. It is heartening that some now teach that all vocations - religious, marriage, and career are equally pleasing to God. Finding that I am no less in God's eyes whether acknowledged by church or not, is terribly important to my self-esteem. I don't regret the years I spent working for and with the church as I see a side of myself developed that might not have been fed, yet

I cannot help but wonder when or if the church will fully recognize the cry of Vatican II; the laity are the People of God. They are the church. (Pg. 488 The Documents of Vatican II, Laity) All people need to be treated equally, laity and clergy alike, all striving to advance God's kingdom here on earth to the best of our ability.

One of the ways to advance God's kingdom is to keep up past relationships. My eighth-grade girl friends, Margaret and Shirley came to my eightieth birthday party; Madeline has passed away. The

My 8th grade graduation.

old Girl Scout song still applies, "Make new friends, but keep the old. One is silver and the other gold!"

Shirley, me and Margaret.

Mother's Day / Feast of the Ascension Reflection May 8, 2016

It seems to me we can consider both of these events as days set aside to remind us to be more loving—towards our earthly mothers, toward Jesus and His Father.

As we hear the reading from Acts tell the apostles to wait a few days till they will be baptized with the Holy Spirit, we can imagine ourselves standing in that group around Jesus. In just a few days the Holy Spirit did descend on all, and now because of that event, we here in this church have also been baptized with this Holy Spirit. Being baptized makes all the difference in our lives as it gives us the grace and strength to live out our choices. Jesus has always chosen LOVE. He came here because his Father asked him to come and show the world a more compassionate merciful God, his Father. God also needed Him to come to show us how to LOVE, to be an example of LOVE, i.e. one who does the will of the God willingly. So, he came as a baby—how better to teach us humans to love? And in coming as a baby, he asked mothers to be the first to love us and by their example to teach us to LOVE.

Every baby comes from within us and so did Jesus. He came from within Mary and from God the Father. If God is to be found in each of us, the task is especially easy when one is looking at a baby. Others will say LOVE is not a baby. They will say Jesus is most like LOVE when he suffered without complaint and gave His life for us. But babies ARE a gift of Love; from God and of God and they point us back to God. In today's Feast of the Ascension, we see Jesus complete the circle by returning, after 33 years as a human, to His Father.

For me, one example of being brought back to God was when we were living in Fresno. It was our second move in two years. We had bought a big house but it was filthy! John had already been transferred on to Brentwood so was only home on Saturday nights; it was just our six kids, a very dirty house, and me. I was pushed, so I pushed the children. One night while putting them to bed, my eight-year-old said, "Mom, all we want is for you to love us." I had missed the mark badly. That night I heard my daughter's voice, but the words were God's, "All I want is for you to love me."

When we are younger, we think love is complete with the coming of new life in a child or in the remembering of Christ's LOVE — by priests in the mass at the consecration, turning bread and wine into Christ's body and blood. As we grow older, we realize LOVE constantly demands MORE, one more act of kindness to a bothersome little brother, a bossy big sister or an irritating neighbor; a little more patience with those closest to us at the end of a long day, more understanding of our adult children living a lifestyle foreign to us. And for our clergy, one more trip to the hospital in the middle of the night to bless the dying or giving time to listen to a parishioner with a complaint about "how things could be done better around here." We realize all our God-given gifts are to be returned with interest no matter the cost. We do get discouraged and wish things had turned out better. I remember when we had four teenagers and one of them made a terrible choice. It could have been tragic so when we were talking it over and explaining what the consequences could have been and how she might have made a different choice, she lamented, "Oh Mom, I must be adopted. Your child would not have messed up so badly."

And isn't that how we sometimes talk to Jesus? "I must not be yours or I would not have made such a bad choice." But Jesus, like a good parent, says you have only to ask and I will help you. We will put some safeguards in place so you don't make this mistake again and together we will get through this.

A few years ago, there was a movie set in India where the hotel guests were always complaining about something. The owner's stock answer was, "Everything will be alright in the end, if it's not alright, it is not yet the end."

Each of us is on his or her own trajectory living out our choices, hopefully going back to God. Maybe, like Jesus, some will leave us early and we will be very sad. But most will see us older ones leave, knowing we are following our stream of light - our journey of LOVE back to the Father, the God of LOVE - love meaning all-knowing, all-accepting, and whole. Here I quote J.P. Newell's book The Rebirthing of God, "The cross of Jesus shows us what we are capable of, that we can LOVE even those who are most opposed to us. This is not our ego's capacity. It is our soul's capacity."

When the tough times come, there is not much strength in our petty small self. Real strength comes from our greater generous Self at the very heart of our being. And herein lies the mystery - the deeper we go into our heart to make a greater effort to love, the further we ascend toward the God of our heart—our Father in heaven. Today we celebrate Jesus' completion of His journey, His Ascension. We also celebrate our mothers who hopefully have shown us how to love. Have faith—our own ascension is yet to come!

March 1, 2020.

Being Blessed

Being blessed is hard to explain
When amid difficult times one has lain.
Yet horrors, nightmares, evil thoughts recede
As darkness into dawn begins to bleed.
Those things that had been trying our sleep to mar
Are no match for joyful light chasing shadows near and far
Bringing with it Hope—for which there is no substitute!
Would that we always felt it near, our fears to mute!

In life there are those who seek to destroy our aspirations,
Who would uncivilly cast aspersions on our precious ambitions.
How cruel not to see, at least to look
That living life, when following the Good Book
Is valid and can add to the richness from which we came
To a place where how you live matters more than your name.
Respecting each other, celebrating our distinctness,
Is the only way to preserve our uniqueness.

Hope born of faith and love
Permeates us from its source above.
I see it as the silver lining of blessing
That can deflect all arrows aimed at our well-being.
It allows us to continue to dream and to aspire
Toward the great heights our gifts inspire.
It is both our task and our offering to human kind,
That the wisdom gained be passed to those behind.

Memoirs

Tony Hoagland explains well why people write their memoirs: they are a reminder of "how life always moves on and yet leaves something behind as well with something alive inside it." That's how I would like to be remembered! That "something" I want to leave is "a spirit" of joy, of can do, of persistence when the going gets tough! It's not to say "do it my way or heed my rules." Oh No! But perhaps "that something" of my life told in my stories will prompt a roar of laughter or a glistening tear in the corner of someone's eye. And then the recognition will dawn that things are not so different as when Grandma lived. Things are different — the lessons are cloaked in different shapes, colors and events. These are still the primary ways to ensure success — tell the truth, to yourself and others; enjoy beauty where you find it, in nature and in others; strive to make things better for yourself and others by being positive whenever possible and remember that mercy, kindness, humor and patience are all necessary to negotiate one's way up to the light.

The lessons in life come to some through others, for some through books, for still others through quiet time alone when the imagination can grapple with life's conundrums without interruption and thus come to innovative means of solving tricky problems. In this process, all our senses are needed; to see, hear, smell, touch and even at times, to taste. Our uniqueness dictates our response to the tests and situations we face. It is said that the first half of life is to be spent following the rules so as to build a strong and complete container or identity for ourselves. The second half of life is to use the container to hold what works for us; to launch ourselves from it to another bigger platform and eventually realize why we are really here, what it is we want to leave. The whole proposal is hypothetical and works differently for each of us. The saving grace is that we are each a work in progress and absolutely no one knows the future or how things will end. It seems best to continue, and to gather awareness as we go rather than stagnate. Hopefully we will be both surprised and approving of who we become, the lessons we've learned and what our purpose has been. May our life energy continue to move us toward that "something we wish to leave that has something alive inside it."

What we are is God's gift to us.
What we become is our gift to God.

— Eleanor Powell

Made in the USA
Las Vegas, NV
24 December 2021

39330571R00175